The Writings of Antonio
Vol. III

The Writings of Antonio Vol. III

US Presidents, Their Generals, and Their Wars

Antonio A. Sweeney

iLearn Research and Consulting Firm

CONTENTS

CONTENTS

CONTENTS

ISBN: 978-1-7349934-7-9 (Paperback)

ISBN: 978-1-7349934-8-6 (eBook)

Library of Congress Control Number: 2020907506

This book is a work of non-fiction.

Front cover image by Artist: Free-Photos @ Pixabay

Book design by Designer: Antonio A. Sweeney

Printed by Ingram Spark and KDP @ Amazon.com

First printing edition 2020.

iLearn Research And Consulting Firm

Phoenix, Arizona 85051

authorsweeney2020@gmail.com

To Follow and See other Books by Antonio go to: amazon.com/author/Antonio.

Other Books by Antonio

The Writings of Antonio Vol. I
(Witty, Philosophical, Political and Sometimes Controversial Commentary on Scripture)
The Writings of Antonio Vol. II
(Philosophical and Political Commentary)
How Scott Walker Became A Spy
(Ghost Writer Spy Novel Series Vol. I)
To Follow and See other Books by Antonio go to: amazon.com/author/antonio.

(To get to author page, type in link just as, period at the end included.)

Society in General
and
The Curious and Thirsty for Historic Knowledge
To the Historian, Scholar, and Student
To the Prophet and the Priest
And Every Statesman
And to my Kids:
Imani, Nathan, Ophelia, and Sonia

5

Well, here we are, another volume of, "The Writings of Antonio." The idea to write this book came to me in light of the current situation with Iran. Just days ago, President Trump ordered military strike upon Iranian General Qasem Soleimani, as he was executed, along with another key official, by our air to ground missile strike on their entourage headed for no good. I sit watching the overview of our intelligence gathering and reports from current video streams provided by national news sources, and strategy overview moving forward,-- given by Secretary of State, Mike Pompeo; and I thought to myself, "Man, this is pretty serious, and I need to start paying more attention."

I mean, I was a junior in college at UCSD, during 9/11 and the Bush Administration, and I don't recall what I was doing when Osama Bin Laden was killed during Obama's term in Office. Nevertheless, today at 39, I think I need to do a better job of keeping up with the currents. Immediately, I acknowledged my own gap in knowledge in terms of US Presidential history as well as War Strategies implemented with and by their Secretaries of State officers for our country. I thought a little study was necessary and I might benefit from taking and producing some notes along the way. Hence, Book 3 of the series, The Writings of Antonio Vol. III, (*US Presidents, Their Generals, and Their Wars.*)

This study will not be comprehensive of all the domestic, economic, and sociological issues going on during each President's term, but will try to focus on major foreign policy decisions with respect to the various Wars fought by our nation at home and abroad, and if at all possible the strategies enacted by our administration to be victorious. I hope I am not biting off more than I can chew, and understand that my analysis or summation will be limited by my lack of access to certain classified and military documents.

Chapter 1

George Washington

Well, here we are, the beginning of a journey through the study of the office of the American Presidency focusing on the wars under their leadership and administration. More specifically, the Presidents role as well as the role of their Secretary of State, weather minor or significant. Coincidentally, many of the Presidents had more than one Secretary of State serve during their term, so in an attempt to not be convoluted in my writing, I will try to be as concise as possible.

George Washington was born on February 22, 1732, and this is the day, or the third Monday of the month rather that we honor Wshington's and Lincoln's birthday's for President's day, which was first officially recognized and celebrated in 1968. A little off topic for this book, but inflight of the fact that I will not be talking much or focusing on the Atlantic Slave Trade or domestic issues during these periods of history, I would also like to highlight Carter G. Woodson, an African American educator, writer and Harvard Graduate, who pushed to implement a Black History Week, also in the month of February. Because of his initial efforts, all of the US Presidents since 1970, have recognized February as "Black History Month."

Under President Washington's administration, aside from the Seven Year's War, which was a global war, so speak, that expanded 5 continents and included multiple European Nations, Africa, India and the Philippines, there were pretty much one other war that we fought. Two major wars, many battles and squirmiest, that I will not go into. but they were obviously, the *French and Indian War (1754–1763)* and the *American Revolution War (1775–1783)*.

The French and Indian war is considered essentially the American sphere of the Seven Year's War as America consisted of colonies of Britain and France, as well as allied Indians, or Native Americans.

The American Revolution was the historic battle of the 13 colonies against King George and the Great Britain Monarchy. Those in the states felt a bit taken advantage of because of the taxes levied by the crown, and ironically coined the phrase, "no taxation without representation." Sounds like a modern day rap lyric. As we fought for our Independence in battle with Great Britain, France came to our aide with money, resources, and Army and Navy reinforcements. French Naval ships were a major contribution to the sea front theater, as they blocked British navy from arriving and taking American ports.

There were four Secretaries of State that served during Washington's term. The first being John Jay, who was born on December 23, 1775 and was maternally home schooled until sent to an Anglican Priest for 3 years and then eventually went off to what is now Columbia University in his early teenage years. He ultimately studied law, started his own practice and among other details, found himself in the seat of the Secretary of State. Secretary John Jay implemented and pioneered a number of operational considerations to strengthen the colonies as a fledgling nation, as well as initiated a currency and credit system that could be recognized by certain European banks.

The second person to fulfill the role of the Secretary of State position under the Washington's administration was Thomas Jefferson, who also served as the third President. Jefferson served as an ambassador to France where he attempted to assist the French and negotiate with Britain on their behalf and interests. Also, there was dispute between Hamilton and Jefferson. Jefferson sought to expand a democratic –republic and was contrary to major banks having so much power in the colonies. Jefferson's education was very broad and he had a depth of many subjects. He started out by reading books from his father's library, and ultimately studied, history, philosophy, the classics, metaphysics, multiple science disciplines, agriculture, law, and even architecture.

Edmund Randolph was the third Secretary of State that served under Washington. Before his career on the president's staff he served as the Attorney General in the state of Virginia. Randolph filled the Secretary of State position after the resignation of Jefferson and worked heavily on the Treaty of Amity or the Jay treaty in which trade, commerce and, navigation between the US and Britain was encouraged. Randolph was known to be a man of peace in light of the ongoing tension between Jefferson and Hamilton.

Timothy Pickering was born on July 17, 1745 and was a Harvard Grad. His politics can be described as opposite that of Jefferson, as he aligned with the Hamilton sentiment on the Federalist papers and in his own right was willing to go to War with France.

Chapter 2

John Adams

The second president of the soon to be independent nation was John Adams. President Adams, helped bring the Revolutionary War to a close and thus was the first president to administrate under a completely independent nation, without Great Britain on its back. Adams was trained as a lawyer, politician, and diplomat. As President he also fought against France in the Quest War (1798-1800).

After winds from the American Revolution settled, Adams found himself in another battle because the French attacked and stole a US ship off the east coast. This led to the legislative branch developing a Navy Department and for other officers to strengthen Army. This happening is ironic to me, considering we sent ambassadors to the French;==namely Jefferson, and secondly, France came to our aide in war against the British helping to establish our independence.

Once again in office, Timothy Picking also severed as Secretary of State during Adam's tenure. This time around, he supported close ties with Britain and as the UK Britain allied with France during the Napoleon Wars (1803-1815). One policy implemented under Picking's leadership was the Embargo Act of 1807, which was an embargo against any and all foreign nations that had intent to do harm to Britain or France during the Napoleon Wars. What's interesting is how quickly our allies changed from President to President.

Charles Lee was the second secretary of state under Adams, but His term was less than a year as he served longer as the US Attorney General (1795-1801)

John Marshall was the third Secretary of State and was given the responsibility to bring the Quasi War to an end. He accomplished this mission and later went to serve as a Chief Justice on the Supreme Court.

9

Chapter 3

Thomas Jefferson

As we see, the founding fathers often served in multiple government roles throughout their legal and political careers. Jefferson served in four main capacities, that is a member of congress, Minster to France, Secretary of State, and herein, President. I know that upon introduction I said that I would not touch on domestic economic issues, yet I think it should be noted that upon taking office, Jefferson took on a national debt of upward 80 million dollars and brought it down to under 60 million through a number of budgetary cuts, maneuvers and downsizing of certain government offices; one such department being the Navy at the time considered by Jefferson in some ways to be unnecessary at it's current size during times of peace.

Interestingly enough, under Jefferson's leadership, America would fight a war on the Seas because of Pirates in those days raiding our ships and taking hostages and bounty, causing conflict. This war would be called the Barbary War, which was against Tripoli a major city of Libya, and Jefferson ordered Navy forces to overtake them upon the Mediterranean Sea.

Something else worth mentioning was that Jefferson saw a need to establish military colleges where our own countrymen could study, amongst other things, topics like engineering that we would not have to have to depend so heavily upon foreign intelligence and ability from individuals who may not be as loyal. The resulting University that precipitated from this idea or Military Peace Establishment Act, was The United States Military Academy or West Point.

The first Secretary of State to serve under Jefferson was Levi Lincoln Sr. He, like many statesmen was a Harvard Graduate and also attained a law degree. Secretary Lincoln was known to be particular when Jefferson wanted to declare war during the Barbary War, and recommend he first get permission from Congress. He also served as the United States Attorney General.

The second acting Secretary of State under Jefferson was James Madison. He was known to have a philosophical bent and helped write the federalist papers. Until now, I have not mentioned the Louisiana purchase, Madison was said to be the Supervisor of this matter.

Chapter 4

James Madison

We have covered Secretary of State Madison, and now we take a bit deeper look at his background and the war his administration was entangled with. To pick up from that which was aforementioned, that he was known to be philosophical, upon Completion of his studies at Princeton, He continued his education into political theory and political philosophy. He learned mathematics, Latin, Greek, and theology as a youth and young adult.

In terms of warfare, Madison had to endure attacks on US eastern shores from Britain and their constant strategic economic means of subversively affecting the colonies thorough industry and commerce. Madison had strategies of his own, one being to attempt to pit Britain against France, and then sent means of delegation officers to Russia to have them arbitrate peace between the two sovereign nations. When these attempts weren't enough, Madison ultimately motioned to Congress for a declaration of War in 1812. It is thought that this was a type of second "war of Independence," And from the outside looking in, it seems that it was fought because Britain was trying to be a bit of a bully at the time, not letting go, even after the Revolutionary War was fought and won.

The First acting Secretary of State under Madison's administration was Robert Smith. He ultimately graduated from Princeton and went on to practice law in the Northeastern part of the Country. He had two major appointments; well I guess three, during his journey to becoming. He served as Secretary to the Navy, and then served in the capacity of

Attorney General from, and finally Secretary of State. He was also was an Army Veteran himself, in combat during the Revolutionary War, under President Washington.

The second Secretary of State serving under President Madison was James Monroe. He was born April 28.1758 and was said to attend school only part time throughout the year because of his families need for him at home on the farm. After graduation from college, he eventually served as Congressmen, Senator, Governor of Virginia, Ambassador to France, Secretary of State, and President.

In the capacity of Secretary of State, he opposed Britain and French attacks on the eastern shores as did Robert Smith. Further, he tried to enact a treaty of which Britain refused to keep compliance, hence the War of 1812. He encouraged Navy Ship attack strategies to go on the offensive and move away from homeland ports. Eventually the Treaty of Ghent was signed by US and Great Britain which ended the War of 1812, and essentially legislated that the two sovereign nations would keep to their own borders.

Chapter 5

James Monroe

As we spoke of Monroe's tenure as Secretary of State, he also served two terms as President of the United States from 1817-1825. Some of the highlights to his foreign policies were continued relations with Britain and he attempted to increase 'trade" between the two nations. Further, a treaty with Russia was also developed to limit Russia's Pacific Boarders.

Domestically, the Missouri comprise was signed, more infrastructure and federal involvement with roads and canals, increase in interstate commerce, and their was a "Panic of 1819 due to an economic slump. I didn't want to make this book another saga about slavery, but I think this is worth mentioning. Under the Tallmadge Amendment, the further introduction of slavery was not permitted into the territory of Missouri, and Children of slaves in that day were considered free at the age of 25.

This is probably cake for the average high school student, but silly me, slept through my US history class in high school, because (and this is not an excuse) it was my Senior year, right after P.E. and lunch and I was a growing, stripling of a teenager with hormones oozing out of my ears. This is no shot to the teacher of course, he was actually great, fun, and interesting, We are still friends on Facebook to this day, he published a book; *Harvest*, by Cris Earnest Nelson. I read it.

I was also in the middle of applying for college and completing my AP Bio-Chem project in the category of Medicine and Health in which

I shared 1st place with my classmate Katy Tom, in the 44th Annual San Diego County Science Fair. Our Bio-Chem class, taught and led by Mr. Larry Nordel, teacher of the Year that year and multiple years in the pass, for the whole state of California Nordel had a number of students that won and went on to The California State Science Fair. I didn't place, but it was an honor to be there with my Scripps Research Institute project on Exposing Pregnant Adult Mothers (rats) to Alcoholic Vapors and determining if their progeny would be more susceptible to alcohol addiction. The guy that was presenting next to me was Asian and had a project from Stanford.

Anyway, back to the topic, John Graham was the first secretary of state to serve under Monroe's administration; He was a Columbia University Graduate, diplomate, and also Minister to Portugal.

Richard Rush was the second acting Secretary of State under Monroe's administration. Rush served as Attorney General before he served as Secretary of State. He was known for his good relations with Britain and also neutralizing the border between US and Canada.

John Quincy Adams was the third Secretary of State under Monroe's administration, among other things. He also served as a Senator, and Minister to Russia, and eventually served in the office of Presidency. In the capacity of Secretary of State he handled issues of keeping the America out of further costly war events with other major Western Powers. He further handled the Latin American affairs of the day, taking a middle line position on their quest for Sovereignty.

Chapter 6

John Quincy Adams

Well, we covered some of Adams achievements in his political career and under the Monroe administration. And yet further, he was educated as a young man, studied Greek, Latin, and French, and ultimately graduated from Harvard like a number of the Presidents before him. In the office of President, he was instrumental in the development of the Naval Academy as well as the National Astronomical Observatory. In terms of War, there were no serious arms conflicts, but more so economic policies over international trade relations with Britain and the West Indies.

As President Adams transitioned from Secretary of State to President, his cabinet member and first acting Secretary of State Daniel Brent only held the position for three days.

The Second Secretary of State to serve under Adams administration was Henry Clay. He was instrumental in developing Latin American foreign relations and attempted to make the French submit payments for their mistrust and attacks during certain war time events. Another one of his goals was to make sure that no other European nation had the upper hand on trade held in juxtaposition with the United States.

Chapter 7

Andrew Jackson

Andrew Jackson was born on the 15th day of the month of March 15, in 1767. He worked saddling horses as a youth and eventually went on to serve in the capacity as an Army General. Domestically, Andrew Jackson implemented new rules for working in government affairs. He required certain merit based accomplishment to hold office, and also released a number of civil servants from their duties because of fiscal irresponsibility. He also was said to hold investigations against the federal government to root out any corruption. Sounds like the FBI before the FBI.

With respect to Foreign Dealings during the Jackson administration, US-French relations were already tense when Jackson came into power. As the aforementioned attacks on American ships on Eastern shores and even further some ships were captured, sent to Spain and men held hostage. Jackson stood firm on holding a stern view toward France because of their government's refusal to make right the debt to America for the past infractions. It is also believed that France was unable to pay due to their own government's finical ruin and insufficiency of funds.

The first Secretary of State to serve under the Jackson administration was Martin Van Buren. It was only for a month and a half, that Van Buren was serving in this capacity; nevertheless he was effective in retrieving some payment from France for past damages.

The third Secretary of State to serve under Jackson, was Edward Livingston Secretary Livingston held a number of positions before serving as the Secretary of State. Also, he was educated as a lawyer, served as a councilman, and further in the office of the Secretary of State he closed the case on the French dealings at the command of President Jackson.

The following Secretary of State after Livingston was Louis McLane. He led in a number of offices before he reached the office of Secretary of Dtate, one of them being Senator. In Jacksons cabinet, he assisted in handling some of the baking issues as well as lobbied to keep tariffs during dealings with South Carolina.

The last Secretary of State to serve under Jackson was John Forsyth. He like many before him served in a number of positions after his graduation from what is now Princeton University. He was a council member in the House of Representatives, held a Senate position, went on to Governor, and finally appointed by Jackson as Secretary of State. Although it was a different time in those days, unfortunately, Forsyth was an advocate of slavery as well as wrote documents pushing forward the Indian Removal Act of 1830, which was a policy that removed Native Americans into Federal territory.

Chapter 8

Martin Van Buren

Mr. Van Buren served as governor, Senator, and Secretary of State, before his post as President of the United States. He studied law, like most politicians was an advocate of reform in which he wanted to change the party system. He opposed ideas motioned by John Quincy Adams on increased federal funding for internal maintenance and upgrade. In terms of foreign affairs, there were a number of squirmishes in Canada with Britain over US-Canadian Border.

John Forsyth was the only Secretary of State to serve during Van Buren's time in office. As we spoke of his dealings under the Jackson Administration, he was party to the Amistad case; a case where African slaves rebelled upon a Spanish ship. The court proceedings involved both US and international law and for more details, consider reading the book or view the movie *Amistad*.

Chapter 9

William Henry Harrison

`William Henry Harrison had the shortest presidency out of all the US Presidents due to an untimely death due to pneumonia. Yet and still, he had a full life of service and duty as he was educated in Greek, Latin, French, logic, and debate as a youth, went on to a boys boarding school and then attended medical school until his tuition was unbearable, and he enlisted into the Army and eventually had a Campaign and was inaugurated as President in 1841.

Domestically and Internationally, Harrison was recorded to push the America Banking System that would align with federalist ideology. The main ideas asserted for American Banking under Clay\'s *American System*, was Tariffs to help with industry, International baking to ease and generate Foreign banking relations, and Federal subsidies to assist with domestic infrastructural.

The first acting Secretary of State under Harrison only served two days and he was Jacob L. Martin. He was the Chief Clerk of he US State Department and was only acting as the Secretary State until the next appointment.

That appointment was none other than, Daniel Webster who started his political career as a lawyer, councilman, then senator, and ultimately Secretary of State, in two administrations. Webster did not do much in terms of Foreign affairs, during the year of 1839 under the Harrison administration besides attend a Whig Convention in Europe.

Chapter 10

John Tylor

President John Tyler, before he was US President, was born on March 20, 1790 and served as a Speaker for the House of Delegates, State court Judge and Governor. He served one other judgeship that was significant and, and moved into the Presidency. At home, Tyler disagreed with Whigs on Banking some banking issues, and motioned for an increase of Tariffs.

In terms of International affairs, Tyler sent a number of diplomats to various nations a generate increased multinational markets and commerce. Nations such as Britain, Berlin in Germany, China and even Huawei. Ultimately six, different Secretaries of State served under President Tyler's administration and leadership.

The first being one who also served under President Harrison's tenure was once again Daniel Webster. During Webster's tenure, there was not much foreign relations that are recorded but domestic economic issues that in which he had a role in.

Hugh Legare was the second acting Secretary of State under President Tyler. He studied law and belonged to a literary society. He also served as a Council Member of the House and eventually an Attorney General. In the position of Secretary of State, he opposed South Carolina's great adversarial attempt to ignore legislation enacted in 1832 that asserted Tariffs.

The next acting Secretary of State was the politician Wiliam C. Derek who only held the position for three days.

The fourth Secretary of State, non=acting, but actually held the position after Daniel Webster, was Abel P. Upshure. He held a number of positions including assisted in leadership with the Navy, and as Secretary of State worked on domestic issues such as dealing with statesmen in Texas to merge with the rest of the country. Further he worked on US-Canada border policy that was settled on his account posthumously.

It seems that during this period of time in US history, America was still becoming a country, annexing states and settling economic issues amongst states and other nations. It was not so much in it's infancy, but maybe it's adolescence with puberty soon approaching, the looming rage of hormonal and emotional craze of the civil war But until then, more domestic issues of formation, annexation, merges, and lines drawn in the sand defining borders, taxation, the shaping of economic policies, and party relations; the seizing of power by lawyers and politicians; the adolescent definition of US government and political science.

The fifth secretary of state after the death of Upshur under President John Tyler's administration was John Nelson. He served about a month after he was appointed Attorney General as well as a councilmen in the House. Like many of his predecessors he was also a lawyer.

John Calhoun was the sixth Secretary of State to serve under Tylor. Before this appointed to this position he was in the House of Representatives, he was the Secretary of War, and then Secretary of State. Secretary Calhoun was instrumental in dealing with the annexation of Texas. Apparently, Texan officials had security concerns with regards to Mexico. With this addition to the Union, Security was expected. To come with the package. It also can be noted that Calhoun was pro=slavery and those issues also played a factor.

Chapter 11

James Polk

James Polk attended University of North Carolina, Chapel Hill and as he progressed through his legal career as President he had a firm agenda in which he wanted to do; one being slice tariffs, and to re-establish the independent treasury system. He also wanted to move forward with bringing Organ and California into the territory. In terms of foreign affairs their were the diplomatic dealings with Britain and the opposition that the territories faced acquiring California from Mexico.

Secretary of State James Buchanan was the only one to serve in this capacity during President Polk's time in office. He was a lawyer, and served as both a Council member to the House of Representatives as well as the Senator of Philadelphia. He later served as a Minister to Russia in the cabinet of Andrew Jackson. Buchanan held all these positions before Serving as Secretary of State, further, as we will discuss later, he was also elected as President.

In the capacity of Secretary of State, domestically Buchanan was an advocate for the addition of the slave-state Kansas. He was also thought to have such an ambition for the office of Presidency that he really over-extended himself to gain territory further Westward from Mexico. After the Mexican–American War. Moreover, together, Polk and Buchanan essentially doubled the territory of the Union, especially with its annexation of Organ.

Chapter 12

Zachary Taylor

Zachary Taylor was born on the 24th day of November in the year of 1784. Unlike other presidents and Secretaries of State, he did not have much of a legal career, but was more so one who served in the military. He was in the war of 1812 among other battles, like the Black Hawk War and the office of the Presidency the Mexican American War. It was probably for his distaste for politics ironically being the president, that he steered away from Congress during his term in office.

In terms of foreign matters under President Taylor's administration; there were concerns with Cuba and Spain. It has been said that Taylor as well as his Secretary of State, whom we will highlight, did not have experience in International affairs. In terms of Cuba, there was an idea of annexing this "slave state" but Taylor and his cabinet found Cuba's leader to be corrupt because of numerous bribery attempts to American military officials. In terms of Spain, Americans were captured through sea militia scourges, but were ultimately returned because Spain did not want a war with America.

Slightly different background than President Taylor, Secretary of State Clayton had practiced law prior to his time in office. He was an advocate domestically for a number of government infrastructure offices, like the Post office in the Washington, DC, and Military affairs Militia, serving on their boards, bringing leadership to their administrations.

Chapter 13

Millard Filmore

Millard Fillmore, 12th president of the United States of America, was born on the 7th day of January in the year 1800. He grew up from humble means, and with hard work and determination became a lawyer and well known attorney in Buffalo, New York. Filmore's international affairs are discussed below with Webster's advances, but he was also instrumental in breaking up the Whig part., He was an advocate of protecting the Union and opposed immigration, nonetheless, his methodology of going about doing these things is ambiguous.

Daniel Webster was the second Secretary of State under Filmore, after Clayton under President Tylor. This would also be his second time holding this office. More that likely for some of these reasons, Fillmore gave him the leadership role in his presidential cabinet. In terms of Foreign policy, Webster opened up avenues of trade between US and Japan. This was an accomplishment considering Japanese "no contact" policy at the time with respect to international trade relations. Further, Webster and Filimore made significant efforts to protect Latin America and Cuba from British imperial aims.

Charles Magill Conrad was the third Secretary of State. He served in a number of positions before and after he took charge of the War Department under President Filmore. He was a cabinet member in the House of Representative, served in the Senate, as well as served in the Confederate of Congress aster time serving in the staff of the executive office. He was a lawyer, and although he served on the war department from 1050-1853, He was later involved on various committees at large during the Civil war years.

Edward Everett was the fourth Secretary of State who served in Filmore's administration. He also like many of his predecessors held many unique positions before his time in the Secretary of State office. Namely he was a Pastor and served as President of Harvard University, taught Greek history and also was a statesmen. Domestically, there were a number of concerns and policies supported by Secretary Everette. It can be noted that he was not for slavery progressing into the Western territories. In terms of foreign affairs. There was political currents that turned some of former Secretary Webster's policies, namely with Japan and with respect to Cuba. Ultimately, American saw Cuba as a concern and wanted it as an independent Sovereign state.

Chapter 14

Franklin Pierce

President Franklin Pierce served in various capacities along his journey to the Oval Office. During his early years, he went to a type of boarding school to prep for college. After college He studied law for one year, and then had a tutelage under a judge where he was admitted to the bar. He was a congressman in both the House of Representatives and the Senate and then the Presidency. Unfortunately during the first weeks of his tenure in office, He was in a horrible train accident. The silver lining in this is that later on during his administration, He had his Cabinet Secretary of Treasure move toward allocating funds for a building infrastructure for travel by way of train across country.

In terms of foreign affairs during President Pierce's time in office, He made efforts towards those in cabinet level ambassador and leadership positions to distinguish themselves as American as opposed to European, especially with respects to dress and the long dark robes. There were also talks of those in consulate positions to be American citizens. Also, no major wars besides the Crimean war (1853-1856), which was primarily on the other side of the pond so to speak. It seems that there were Britain recruiters in the US enlisting American's for this war. This was primarily Russia's war, where they lost the Aliant forces of the Ottoman Empire, France, Britain, and Sardinia. It was a battle over Christians and Holy land.

The acting Secretary of State who served as an assistant was William Henry Jr. The next official Secretary of State was William L. Mercy. He was a graduate of Brown University and went on to have a political and military career. He practiced law, held a House position as well as served in the Senate. He was a captain and war fighter, and ultimately served as the Secretary of State in Pierce's Administration. Under his leadership,

Secretary of State Mercy also, in terms of Foreign Affairs was instrumental in purchasing Sothern parts of New Mexico and Arizona from Mexico. These were some of the last territories to be added to the United States. And finally there were economic dealings with Great Britain as to their possessions in Canada. A treaty was formed to legislate policy in this matter.

Chapter 15

James Buchanan

The fifteenth President of the United States of America was none other than James Buchanan. He was thought to be a bit of a class act, but finished his preparatory studies at the Stone Academy and pursued graduate level vocation after his time at Dickerson College. He also performed his civic duty in the War effort around 1814 as a private. Like many high officials He not only had a legal career, but served as Ambassadors to both Russia and the United Kingdom. He also served in the House and the Senate.

In terms of Foreign Affairs, President Buchanan wanted to change policy with respect to Central America. There was already a treaty in place by way of the Clayton administration, but Buchanan's intent on modification of the treaty was to give the United States a greater reach. Buchanan had other ambitions. He wanted to purchase other territories; among them, Cuba from Britain- to no avail, and Alaska from Russia in which a settlement of price could not be met.

The first Secretary of State to serve under President Buchanan was Lewis "Cass. He was another one to serve as an Army Officer in the War of 1812 in his young adulthood., and later served in Congress. Further history reveals that he was Secretary of War under President Jackson, negotiated various treaties with Native Americans, and served as an Ambassador to France. Like Buchanan, Secretary Cass was also ambitious. He wanted to purchase more land from Mexico, and yet worked on the Clayton Treaty that limited US and Britain powers in Latin America.

William Hunter, Jr was only the acting Secretary of State, a Politician who had served in this position three times. The next Secretary of state was Jeremiah S. Black who attended law school and was a Chief Justice, as well as Attorney General before he was appointed to the position by President Buchanan. One noted act was that he admonished US foreign ambassadors to warn the heads of states of countries they were in not to recognize the Confederacy. There were issues of Constitutionality at home.

Chapter 16

Abraham Lincoln

President Abraham Lincoln, the 16th man to hold the Oval Office of the United States of America. Often known and famed for his abolition of slavery, Gettysburg address, and the aforementioned Emancipating Proclamation of 1863. He also is responsible for preserving the Union, having influence in the upgrading of the economy, and carrying and caring for America through one of it's most brutal and deadly wars, The Civil War, where brother killed brother. He developed himself from impoverished roots and become a self-taught lawyer, with a practice before he entered into politics

It is also documented that President Lincoln exercised his full executive authority in commanding efforts in the Civil War. He restricted military aide to the south, he had confederate sympathizers arrested and jailed, he blocked ports and enlisted men of fighting age from Northern states. It was a gruesome battle where American sons and fathers, fought each other.

I remember the first time I learned the meaning of "civil" war, it kind of struck me. I thought it was just another war, like any other foreign war we fought like World War I or II. And in a way, was it not; because, are we not all brothers of different skin tones, representatives of mankind. Or are we something much different, arriving and deriving from various planetary systems and Worlds, incomprehensible to the natural man, until we retire and return to our God. Houses and Kingdoms fighting upon the earth fulfilling some ultimate or historic destiny, unbeknownst to us. Yet I digress,-- the fact that It means War within a nation amongst the same peoples. A house divided against itself and countrymen of the same nation fighting amongst ourselves to the point of death and murder. Well, History has shown us that "there is nothing new under the son" (Ecc 1:9). And we were not the first nor the last to endure Civil War. Rome, Africa, China, England, Russia, Ancient Israel itself, Syria and the modern day Palestinian-Israeli conflict. Even Ancient Asiatic klans fought for supremacy.

William H. Steward was the first Secretary of State under Lincoln's Presidency. In his early life he experienced travels to the South, tasting it's hospitality and yet witnessing the brutally of slavery, he streamlined back North to complete his undergraduate degree and further, went on to endure law school. As a professional, he was elected governor and later served in the Senate before holding the office of Secretary of State.

In terms of foreign affairs, it is recorded that Secretary Seward would not have resisted war with European powers if they showed recognition to Confederate envoys. But Lincoln held his reigns and relations smoothed over, and America lobbied for the Union in Europe. Lincoln arrested Confederate Envoys that attempted to cross the pond for the same measures.

Andrew Johnson

President Andrew Johnson held many positions before sitting in the Oval Office. Governor, Senator, and Vice President of Lincoln to name a few. In terms of foreign policy, the matters that awaited him when he took office after Lincolns assassination was the French's reach into Mexico. In this matters inception, the French held the support of Britain and Spain, But the United States was firmly against these actions, and scolded the French that they should not mettle with Mexico as well as their affairs.

Although the United States had made treaties and had past Wars with Mexico over southwest territory, our leadership felt that that Mexico was ultimately none of France's concern. Apparently, the reason for the French's thirst for blood was because Mexican leadership stiffed some European creditors with an issue of moratorium on loan payments.

William H. Steward remained in his position of Secretary of State from the Lincoln assassination through the Johnson Administration. He had an expansionist perspective and wanted to gain new territory.

26

Chapter 18

Ulysses Grant

President Ulysses Grant was a war hero who saw combat and lead the Union Army. He fought against Robert Lee who was the Confederate General; and was victorious, it is documented that General Lee conceded in battle. Grant attended the Military Academy at West Point and as he was instrumental in the Union wining the Civil War, two weeks after President Lincoln's assassination Grant found himself in another leadership position as President Johnson, appointed him to be the Army General.

As President, Grant was a proactive and intentional policy maker. He indicted the Ku Klux Klan and advocated for African Americans to realize their freedom and civil rights. After all, that was a major reason why the war was fought. He was not elected a third term, nevertheless, he wrote a successful autobiography that apparently did really well and confirmed his beloved popularity and genuinene favor from the American people for what he had done.

In terms of Foreign Affairs America did not meddle too heavily in that of Spanish rule and dealings with Cuba. As Cuba rebelled, America did not take notice until 8 American prisoners were taken and murdered by Spanish Pirates. American citizens called for war, and President Grant called for the Navy. These dealings were ultimately settled by the Spanish President giving monetary concessions to the American families for the innocent lives taken.

The first Secretary of State to serve under President Ulysses Grant was Elihu B. Washburn. He was independently motivated from the age of 14 and finished school, He began to study law and passed the bar exam. He made partner and served as a Congressmen as well as Minister to France during the Frenco-Prussian war of 1870. This

was a war that established the early Germen empire, and defeated French hegemony in Europe.

The second Secretary of State under President Grant was Hamilton Fish. Secretary Fish was thought to be one of the greats to hold this positon because of his massive efforts toward foreign policy and his effectiveness in establishing new legislation. For instance, he established the international arbitration, which is essentially diplomacy first among nations who are in conflict before taking arms in military action or response. Secondly, he handled the issue of the Union making claims to Great Britain for making Naval ships for the Confederacy. Thirdly, he kept peace with Cuba through the Spanish incident. Fourthly, he attempted to make The Dominican Republic additional US territory, and finally, he attempted to initiate trade agreements with Korea, to no avail. After he served his time in office he retired to his law practice.

Chapter 19

Rutherford B. Hayes

Rutherford B. Hayes was the nineteenth President to hold the oval office of the United States of America. He started off as a practicing lawyer who held the governorship in New York as well as served as councilmen in the House or Representatives before his ascension. As President, Hayes held egalitarian views and a meritocracy base philosophy. He was known to treat all individuals the same, not favoring a man's race, social class, or economic standing, but felt that all men should prove their own worth.

In terms of foreign policy, President Hayes reach stretched to the Suez Canal, as he displayed American interest, wanting to determine that the US not be overruled by European Interest or powers. Secondly he took out Mexican militias that had plans to take root and build Armies on American soil. He ordered US army troops to defeat these militias suddenly. And finally, Hayes upheld a treaty with China that allowed free flow of Chinese trade and immigration into the United States.

Even after the Panic of 1873 and riots in San Francisco in which the population figured that it was due to massive influx of Chinese immigration that caused wage depreciation and depression in US and even European countries. This rose to the Chinese Exclusion act being brought to the forefront by congress, wherein it would have restrained or halted Chinese immigration, a bill that President Hayes vetoed. There was massive backlash, and even an attempt to have him impeached, which did not happen. A similarly written act was ultimately passed after his term in office was complete.

William M. Evarts was the second Secretary of State under President Hayse. After Hamilton Fish continued his service from President Grant's administration. William Evarts was known as an excellent scholar and politician. This reputation for literature and studying law followed him even into where he served as Senator. In terms of Foreign Policy issues during his tenure, there was the issue as to whether or not, he was going to acknowledge the Mexican Government. This quarry of his posed problematic because by refusing to recognize Mexico's, it allowed him to send Army troops after Indian gorilla warriors past the Mexican border.

Secondly, there was still the issue of Chinese immigration, in which the influx of legal Chinese immigrants was significantly restrained. Thirdly, one particular source report that there was corruption within the administration of Foreign Affairs, that he kept quiet about, and refused to report on. Other documentation cast Secretary Evorts as being a peacemaker and trying to mitigate conflict between Peru, Bolivia, and Chili.

Chapter 20

James A. Garfield

James A. Garfield was the twentieth President of the United States of America. He was an English immigrant, whose father died at a young age. Landing in Ohio, he grew up and grew older and attended Seminary before college. In his college years he took an interest to Greek and Latin and graduated with High Honers--Phi Betta Kappa. He worked constantly during his education, and had a few humble positions, such; as mule hand, janitor, carpenter but essentially was a preacher. As an itinerant minister, he had a local circuit and enjoyed preaching for its oratory, argument, and command over audiences.

As president, in terms of foreign relations. President Garfield had on his agenda to increase trade within Western nations, more specially North America with Latin America to restrain Greater Britain influxes in South and Latin America. Secondly, he also had the notion that advancing international trading would bring a feel of prosperity to our own nation. This notion coming from a place that "more is better," considering that in our grandiosity, our nation would be considered prosperous.

Other interesting and unfortunate facts, are that President Garfield was the only Counsel men rising from the House of Representatives to become assassinated and his time in the highest office of State was short lived.

James G. Blaine was the only Secretary of State to serve under President Garfield, and yet held the office for two Presidents. As a young man Blaine accepted a position as a mathematics professor at the Western Military Academy and took to a study of languages. He also had thoughts of law school but ultimately decided upon employment as co=editor with a newspaper publication that aligned with his political regards.

Secretary Blaine was an expansionist and fought to reclaim for American interest and territory. One such example were the American prisoners who were held hostage in Ireland after being arrested and held without trial. Apparently, these captives were released because of the cleverness of Secretary Blaine's negotiative skill and diplomacy. Further, under Garfield's administration, means of peace were brokered between Mexico and Guatemala.

30

Chester Alan Arthur

Chester A. Arthur was the twenty-first President of the United States of America. He took office after the assassination of President Garfield. He served leading a militia during the civil war and went on to practice law. He was appointed and fired from a Collections Post by two different Presidents but this did not dissuade his will, heart and courage to want to serve his country and countrymen in the office of the Presidency.

As an inheritor of a previous Chief Administrator's office and cabinet, there was slight adjustments that had to made because of initial conflict amongst the staff and the new incumbent, as can be with any organizational change an hiring of new leadership. Some cabinet members from the previous administrator left earlier than President Arthur requested. Other citizens holding civil positions had to be removed by Arthur for reasons of their corruption.

In terms of Foreign affairs, there was a 50 cent tax levied on all immigrants, and the immigration act of 1882 was signed by President Arthur which denied criminals, those mentally challenged, and any others potentially dependent upon public assistance.

Frederick T. Frelinghuysen was the next Secretary of State to serve after Secretary Blaine. He was orphaned by the early death of his parents at a young age as they both died, and he spent his youths in the care of his grandparents. He grew up to practice law and serve first as a Politician and Senator, and then Secretary of State. It appears Secretary Frelinghuysen essentially held the position without much ado about anything until President Grover Cleveland took office. Former Secretary Blaine did the heavy lifting under President Arthor before he left.

Nevertheless, there where still matters in Peru, Bolivia, and Chile that Secretary Frelinghuysen handled. He negotiated a peace treaty even though there were still heavy tensions between US and the three South American counties due to lass of land. There were also matters in Europe and also Venezuela that are worthy of noting.

Chapter 22

Stephan Grover Cleveland

Mr. Cleveland, before he was president had the fortune of being educated at two Academies in his youth; Fayetteville, and The Clinton Academy. When it was time for him to attend college, there was a minister from church who offered a scholarship if Young Cleveland would agree to become a Preacher, and the young Mr. Grover knowing himself and his own devices and proclivities, had to decline. In New Youk he held a clerkship and was introduced to a firm by his Uncle. As he began to read the law He was admitted. to the New Youk Bar. After some years, he then served as Mayor then Governor, and ultimately the twenty-second President of the United States.

I know this work focuses mainly on background and then Foreign Policy issues dealt with by US Presidents and Secretaries of State, but when President Cleveland took office, there were apparently many vacancies within the government that needed to be filled. In that case, Mr. Grover began to appoint persons of his will to these offices, and made an agreement that he would not fire any republican that was doing their job already in their position, nor would he hire anyone one on the sole reason of partisan politics. Therefore, some democrats were selected to hold policy making positions, as he was a Democrat himself. We can understand this occurrence as current and recent Presidents have appointed Chief Justices to the Supreme Court during their tenure.

In terms of Foreign Policy, President Cleveland was the opposite of an imperialist and had no real vigorous expansionist ambitions as most leaders do. He took a hands off approach and really handled the domestic matters leaving the Foreign matters to his Secretary of State and cabinet—Namely Secretaries of State: Richard Olney.

33

Chapter 23

Benjamin Harrison

Benjamin Harrison served as the twenty-third President of the United States of America. His was the grandson of a President and attended law school after graduating from college. It is recorded that he networked throughout his life through membership of two fraternal organizations that allowed dual membership; one collegiate, and the other a law fraternity. Before the office of the presidency Mr. Harrison served as a US Senator

In terms of matters of Foreign Policy, it is said that he and his Secretary of State Blaine hade quite an abrasive relationship, but in the end forged together a legislation that was both aggressive and effective. One of the major impetus of President Harrison's goals was to expand the Navy. He thought that this would further protect US from Oceanic attacks and give more of a global presnec.es. Although increased treaties with Latin America were made and Fredrick Douglass sent as Ambassador to Haiti, President Harrison did not succeed in planting a Naval Base in that territory. Further gridlock between the three Nations of

Britain, Germany, and the US over the Samoa islands

William Fisher Wharton served as acting Secretary of State under President Harrison. He was Harvard Educated with back study in Greek, Latin and Ancient History. He graduated law school and was poised for civil leadership. In terms of matters of foreign policy, apparently not much was done, in fact, he is recorded resigning his positon to return to his law practice in Massachusetts.

The following Secretary of State was that of John Watson Foster He was also a Harvard law graduate and in terms of diplomacy delt with the nation Mexico and their leadership.

Grover Cleveland

The twenty-fourth President of the United States was Grover Cleveland. This was his second time in the oval office as the chief executive. This time in terms of foreign policy, Cleveland dealt with an Hawaiian tyrant who opposed constitutional law as well as domestically slightly adopted the Monroe doctrine which disallowed the forming of any European colonies. President Cleveland also doubled the Navy ship count during his second time in office.

The first official Secretary of State to serve under President Cleveland's administration was Walter Quintin Gresham. He was a lawyer who served not as a Senator or Governor, but sat as a Judge. Some foreign affairs that Gresham was apart of was dealing with Great Britain and keeping them out of American official government business. There was a coup attempt that that was exposed by some loyalist. And yet, Grisham allied with Britain to eventually remove a Nicaraguan despot.

The second acting Secretary of State appointed by President Cleveland was Edwin F. Uhl. He studied law as was assigned the task of investigating

American government offices in Europe. Further, there was a later appointed as Ambassador to Germany.

The third appointed Secretary of State of the President Cleveland's administration was that of Secretary Richard Olney. He was also a Harvard law grad with his Bachelor's degree from Boston University. Before he served as Secretary of State he was appointed Attorney General. He was placed in the middle of the Cuban = Spaniard feud as Cuba sought to break away from Spaniard rule. AS Spain tried to resist the Cuban Revolt, US government got involved and later you will find that these actions led to the Spanish – American War. There was also tension between Britain and Venezuela city states such as Guayan, as the imperial power sought for more control and border expansion, the United States intervened as protector.

William McKinley

The twenty-fifth President of the United States of America was non other than William McKinley. At a young age his family moved to Ohio, and he graduated a Seminarian as well as attended college to obtain a Bachelor's degree. He was a member of the Sigma Alpha Epsilon Fraternity. Moving forward in history to the time of foreign policy issues in President McKinley's administration; The fight for Cuban Independence was underway in the year of 1895.

It was the result of years of revolt from Cuba to lift off Spain's colonial hooks on their nation; In these matters, America was Cuba's ally. In attempts to give Cuba aide against Spanish offshore attack, Naval ship USS Maine was sent and sunk by "unknown" forces said to loose over 200 solders. Later when these matters were investigated, the only answer that was come up with was an "underwater mine."

Spain continued to reject President McKinley's attemps at negotiating Cuban Independence and once brought to hs legislative body, we declared war against Spain. During the war efforts, President

McKinley had the luxury of the telephone, which allowed him to communicate with Navy and Army ground troops and be involved, a technology that past presidents did not have access to.

There was a squirmiest on the Caribbean isles. and America was victorious, though we suffered casualties. President McKinley next move was to set his sights upon Puerto Rico with the intent of uprooting Spain. Cuba was already under American Control and after American militias destroyed Spaniard supply ships, Spain was quickly ready to send concessions.

The first Secretary of State to serve under the Mc Kinley administration was the John Sherman had a pretty political career serving three times in the house as well as a number of times in the senate. Not to mention, he served as Secretary treasurer as well. Secretary Sherman was known to have an abrasive relationship with President McKinley in all matters of foreign policy; he was even weak in his support for Cuban acquisition and the Spanish-American War which was fought for Cuban Independence from Spain.

The Second appointed Secretary of state was William Rufus Day. He was actually appointed assistant to Secretary Sherman due to the nature of the tense relationship between President Mc Kinley and Secretary Sherman.

William Day studied law for a year after college and went on to become a Supreme Court Justice. As secretary of State, he bore an inner conflict in his conscious as he wanted to return to Spain all of their fought for territories, including Cuba. Yet he voted and administrated the President's will in continuing support of the Spanish-American War. Due to Secretary Day's diplomatic and negotiating skill and force, he helped in the acquisition of Cuba, Puerto Rico, Guam and the Philippines to America for $20 million dollars.

Alvey Augustus Adee served as the next acting Secretary of State during the Spanish-American war. He had years of service in the state department and even served as an administrative secretary to some past in leading government positions. His role was quite significant though he remained official third in command to the Secretary of State. Secretary Sherman was old and had ill health, and acting Secretary Day was inexperienced, therefore, Secretary Adee found himself in a positon of leadership from behind, managing diplomatic affairs convincingly during the Spanish American War. It was after these happenings that he took the position officially for a short time after Secretary Sherman left office.

John Milton Hay was the final Secretary of State under McKinely administration. He was a graduate of Brown University and went on to take up the study of law afterward. As Secretary of State, he had to handle maters after the Spanish-American War was over, and one key business matter at the time was that of the acquisition of the Philippine Isles. Additionally, there was the settlement of the Alaskan=Canada border issue. Secretary Hay stayed in office, even until President Roosevelt and his new cabinet took leadership

There are other matters such as the dealings with open trade with China, and the initial steps to contracting the development of the Panama Canal, but these facts can be found in another place.

Theodore Roosevelt

Theodore Roosevelt served as the twenty-sixth president of the United States of America and also held some other governing positions before his time in the Oval Office—namely Police commissioner, governor, Vice President, and Assistant Secretary of the Navy. He was a writer, politician, adventurist, warrior and in my opinion an extreme risk taker. President Roosevelt was Harvard educated graduating near the topo of his class; Phi Betta Kappa. Shortly thereafter, he experienced the death of his father, inheriting a significant sum of money for that time, and chose to pursue law school at Columbia University, with the intention of eventually finding a way to get into politics. It should be mentioned that in his undergraduate studies, Roosevelt excelled in philosophy, science, and speech and debate, but struggled with some of the classical languages such as Greek and Latin; Even though he had French and Germen under his belt.

President Roosevelt wrote during his time in law school, a book on the, "War of 1812" as he studied the tracking and war time nautical maneuvers of Navy Ships from official documents.

The first acting Secretary of State to serve under President Roosevelt after Secretary Hayes was Secretary Francis B. Loomis. He replaced Hayes after his death, as had opportunity to have a number of responsibilities before the first World War, including ambassador to "France and Japan. He also handled closing mattes of the Acquisition of the Panama Canal territory.

Elihu Root was next in line to officially take the office of Secretary of State in the Roosevelt administration. His contributions were expansive and significant. Yet, this was not his first go round serving in a government administrative position. From the time of his completing law school and becoming an attorney, he served in both a private and government sectors making broad sweep changes in military affairs as well as representing high dollar corporate clients. Before serving as Secretary of State, He was the Secretary of War and helped renovate the face of the Military in terms of the availability of military schools, advance technology, and professionalism with respect to execution of service, specifically in dealing with Cuba. His responsibilities as Secretary of State led him to negotiate among 24 nations and devote policy to enact arbitration as the protocol to handling international disputes before the detriment of war.

From reading documentation on Secretary Root, in my personal assessment he seemed to be a man of extreme business sense and highly skilled in his ability to completely re-structure and organize at the operational level and down to the point of; whereas, functionality and effectiveness was at a higher level; productivity included. Perhaps this came from wisdom gained from his representation of many senior level corporate clients, in addition to his father being a mathematician.

The final Secretary of State appointed by President Roosevelt, and to serve under his administration, was none other than, Robert Bacon. Secretary Bacon was said to be close friends with Roosevelt and before his appointment as Secretary of State he served as assistant to Secretary Root. He was a Harvard Graduate as well as a graduate of law school. He was documented for leading in the Preparedness committee which helped train and prepare soldiers for World War I, as he himself would also serve in that theatre after his term as Secretary of State.

In terms of Foreign policy, He helped settle matters pertaining to Columbia and the Panama Canal.

38

Chapter 27

William Howard Taft

William Howard Taft served as the twenty-seventh President of the United States of America. He was born in Ohio and graduated from his baccalaureate studies from Yale College. This would spring board his next step, which was attendance at Cincinnati Law School, in which he completed his degree and launched into political, judicial, and eventually executive service.

President Taft was the first President to serve as both Chief Executive Officer and also, afterward in the Judicial branch of government, sitting as a Supreme Court Justice.

In terms of foreign policy, President Taft, in short, was for World Peace. He was not for meddling in European affairs neither did he want them meddling in our affairs. He motioned for the Rule of Arbitration when dealing with matters between Britain and France but Congress balked.

There was only one Secretary of State that served under President Taft and his administration, and that was non other than Philander C. Knox.

Secretary Knox was educated at in public school and graduated college from West Virginia University He went on to serve in the Senate and then as the Attorney General before being appointed to the office of Secretary of State. He had a major hand in American Steel policy formation as a Corporate lawyer before his time in the office of Secretary of State. Further, he was one to innovate policy and make changes to how the department of state was organized, as he implemented the structural change of separating the department in the regional divisions. This type of layout allowed for expertise amongst the officers to be rather easily observed and assigned by the chief officer to various tangential or whatever the problematic issue.

There were some other matters that Secretary Knox handled dealing with the Bearing Strait and saving Killer whales being. slaughtered. He was also on for open and free trade with Latin America, which ultimately pointed to a democratic state as opposed to other forms of government such as communism or socialism.

40

Chapter 28

Thomas Woodrow Wilson

Thomas Woodrow Wilson was the 28th President of the United States of America. He attended college at what is now Princeton University and went on to attend University of Virginia Law school for about one year. Among self study of the law, President Wilson took up a study of political philosophy as well as political history and thought. More of the philosopher at heart, although He possessed a strong administrative gift as he held key leadership positions in college, organizing the college paper, baseball and football leagues., it is recorded that he was board with the day to day routine of holding a legal practice. Ironically, he also served his city as a Professor and College President, so he was used to the daily push and shove of paperwork and dealing with people, and legislating policies.

I don't focus on domestic policies and happenings to much in this book setting, but something worth mentioning for President Wilson was his role in continuing the League of Nations as well as establishing the Federal Reserve Banking system, because of a need for a Central banking system.

In terms of Foreign policy, it seems that President Wilson had many affairs to deal with countries in South America and the Caribbean Isles. There was troops sent to Haiti, moves in completing the Panama Canal to quicken travel and connect the Pacific and Atlantic Oceans.

William Jennings Bryan wss the first Secretary of State to serve in the cabinet of President Woodrow Wilson. He was educated in his younger years in Private School and later went to Illinois College. After graduation, it was off to law school, like so many other leading political figures. During law school he had a fellowship at a local attorney's office and also aided in Chaplin services during his undergraduate career.

Along with President Wilson, Secretary Bryan took serious the task of his domestic and foreign administrative responsibilities. He was key in legislating that the president appoints members of the Governors or Board of Directors of the Federal Reserve, thus establishing a central bank. Also, there within the governing architecture of foreign policy, there was a tribunal contracted to investigate measures that needed arbitration. Mostly all of the foreign powers and assemblies submitted to this judicial body during that time in 1913 before World War I, besides Germany and Austria-Hungary.

Robert Lansing was the second to serve as Secretary of State under President Wilson, and fitted with a significant amount international relations experience due to his role during World War I. He was instrumental in brokering treaties between Japan and America after the War. Secretary Lansing went to law school and worked for a law firm after college.

As we notice, law school seems to be the initiation or bar for entering into the realm of politics and international relations, so many of those appointed to public office have at least achieved or merited to this degree. Others have been Entrepreneurs, Tycoons, Pioneers, and Professional business men/women, or beneficiaries of inherited wealth, who have exponentially grown their finances to a point of prosperity that they could afford to run for public office from their sheer will, adrenalin. and ability. Of course this is the obligation of those interested in Presidential and legislative offices in government.

Some of the actions that Secretary Lansing did was the purchase the Danish West Indies under a treaty. Further actions were involving America and Japan having a fluid trading agreement and open boarder policy. And Finally, there was settling the matters of Japanese interest in China.

I was always under the impression that it was President Edgar Hoover who was the architect of the FBI, and though this be a different organization Secretary Lasing is documented as putting together an investigative Security force, working for the State Department to look in to affairs of Central Powers==Namely, the League of Nations before and during WWI.

Frank Polk was a graduate of Yale College and went on to law school and eventually to practice. He was only the acting Secretary of State for a short time, approximately less than a week and a half. After his short term there was Bainbridge Colby. President Wilson appointed Secretary Colby officially as the third Secretary of State in his administration. Secretary Colby graduated from College and started law school at Columbia Law, and after one year, transferred to New York Law School where he completed his degree. In terms of foreign policy. Secretary Colby and President Wilson had congruent philosophies and a good working relationship. Secretary Colby had the opportunity to work with the Versailles Treaty after the first World War even though the "Big Four" idea was shot down in the Senate. Secretary Colby had better luck in his Latin American travels as his policies promoted Democracy abound.

Chapter 29

Warren G. Harding

Warren G. Harding was the twenty-ninth president of the United States of America. His Educational background is a little vague as he attended grade school and college and law school for one year but that he was admitted into the bar is not recorded. He saved money and purchased a newspaper. He also was a governor and Senator before his ultimate launch to the office of the Presidency. One criticmentioned in so many words that he, President Harding that is, had very loquacious speeches that were filled with superfluous words and phrases, but upon reading one of his quotes, it just seems he rambled on with the intent of creating various thought pictures to communicate his many points and ideas.

In terms of foreign policy and international affairs, President Harding delegating much of that responsibility to Secretary Hughs. His first challenge was to settle matters of post World War I global aftershocks as our Senate had a hard stance rejecting US entry into the league of Nations and we essentially remained in conflict with Germany, Austria, and Hungry until other treaties were signed

Time went on, and US relations with the League of Nations were still sparse, as we would not send ambassadors for political reasons but for technological and humanitarian aid purposes only. As a laymen of politics, it seems at this point we were dogmatic about keeping our sovereignty and autonomy as a nation and always wanting to act unilaterally without the infringement of other nations or a counsel's global legal rule. This is simply my analysis of politics I do not fully understand and my limited knowledge and perspective of that particular history.

There war other matters of German reparations that were to be paid to US. Apparently Germany dragged her feat in our payment and tried to mitigate the payment through a multilateral counsel in which we would have none of. Eventually some other treaty was signed Finally, there were matters of Russia being recognized or unrecognized and aided by US. Matters of US-USSR trade relations that were not fully settled under President Harding's administration.

The only Secretary of State to serve in President Harding's administrative Cabinet was none other than Mr. Charles Evans Hughes. He was formally educated and graduated from the illustrious Brown Universe at the tender age of 18, He had a few notable public offices before being appointed Secretary of State. There was the governorship of

New York, as well as Serving as a United States Supreme Court Justice Associate. Few men and leaders have had the opportunity to traverse the US courts of power from the judicial branch to the cabinet of the Oval Office. Normally, precedence has shown that the majority of Executive Officers matriculate through college, graduate law school, and run for some public office to become a Councilmen or Senator. But the Judicial branch is not one to be elected to, but appointed by the Chief of State; --Presidential appointment.

According to official state documents, Secretary Hughes developed and implemented a number of treaties with more than a few nations during his tenure. He was progressive in his dealings with Latin America, including Mexico and Columbia, as well as proactive with US foreign policy dealings with Japan and Berlin in singing various treaties.

Calvin Coolidge

Calvin Coolidge was the thirtieth president of the United States of America. Before his ascension to the Oval Office, he also served as Vice President and held positions of Governor and Senator. In his youth he was educated at two Academies and later completed law school, eventually practicing commercial law.

Other documentation report President College as having a very dry sense homer, often given to few words, making efforts to speak as less as possible during interviews, giving "yes" and "no." responses, saying "even this is too much, because they just keep going on even longer." In my assessment of the available reports made available by way of the internet, he seems to be curt, yet philosophical, possibly a bit impatient, yet meditative, as he practiced what he in so many words called the art of "doing nothing;," or active inactivity.

So, although he was deemed a Republican and lazze-fair politician, also considered decisive in his actions, he was kind of a middle line guy when it came to governmental role in the life of Americans; as he did not move to aide farmers with government funds, nor did he advocate using Federal powers to stop or break up successful businesses during the prosperity boom of the Roiling 20's. It was this

In terms of foreign policy, President Coolidge took a more reserved approach in dealing with other nations. He was of the opinion that America was great and needed be brought under the rule of any foreign council. Although there was still the decision that needed to be made or whether or not to join the League of Nations, ultimately under President Coolidge's administration, it did not happen. He did consider the World Court as well, but this organization as well, under his administration, America did not join.

Other foreign events under Coolidge administration; Germany still owed US money from WWI, Russia still went unrecognized, and US, Britain, France, Germany, Italy, and Japan supposedly renounced war, In so many words, making an international treaty, that did not completely do away with war but established a relationship between the nations after the pangs of the first World War.

Efforts were made to recognize Mexican government post Wartime. Also considering Latin America elements of peace from America were made as an apology for intervening during maters of Caribbean affairs. President Coolidge also made his one and only foreign affairs visit to Cuba.

Frank B. Kellogg was after Hughes in serving as Secretary of State for the full of President Coolidge term in office. He matriculated through college and law school and actually became the President of a Bar Association. He had one term in the Senate and also was selected for a Special investigations committee before that.

In terms of foreign policy matters, Secretary Kellogg started his job before his term in office first serving as an Ambassador to the United Kingdom. In this vein, he negotiated matters of German reparation payment to Allied nations, still left pending from WWI. Also there were issues in Latin America, more specifically Peru and Chili Border conflicts. It is documented that some 80 treaties were signed by Secretary Kellogg.

What is said to be the most significant policy navigated by Secretary Kellogg was arbitration of Treaties with France. The Ambassador of France and Secretary Kellogg came up with a deal that was to forever cement peace between the two nations. It was readily accepted and ratified by the US senate, but criticized as something that would never hold or prevent war.

Chapter 31

Herbert Hoover

The thirty=first President of the United States of America the Mining Engineer Mr. Herbert Hoover. He served the country in a major capacity before and after his term in the Oval Office. As a Stanford Mining Engineer graduate, Mr. Hoover took off to Cinna with his new wife and ended up in Europe bringing tourist back safely after Germany initiated conflict with France. Later Mr. Hoover served as the Secretary of Commerce and assisted Belgium with Nutritional Aide.

Domestically, President Hoover was known as the "scapegoat of the Great Depression," As the recession of the 30's started during his tenure. But this is not the book or setting for domestic affairs, as I said at the onset, we would highlight foreign policies and International affairs. Mr. Hoover attempted to pull back military action in Latin America. There were still matters of concern to handle in the Dominican Republic and in El Salvador. Apparently some leftist rebellion had aroused and the situation needed to be neutralized with the aide American forces. Nevertheless,

Banana wars were brought to end under his administration as well as occupied territories in Nicaragua, and troops in Haiti were brought home.

There was the period where President Hoover sought for disarmament to prevent the global Naval race. World Naval powers got on board and the London Naval Treaty was signed which was essentially an agreement between the UK, Japan, Italy, and the US to limit and control submarine warfare as well as decrease spending on axillary naval equipment.

As we can see, The Soviet Union was not a part of this particular treaty and still posed an auspicious shadow on global affairs. President Hoover was concerned about Japan's invasion of China in particularly because he felt that US conflict with Japan would deny US another ally against The Soviet Union, which was the greater threat in the grand scheme of things at the time. Notwithstanding, from these matters developed the Stinson Doctrine, in which is stipulated that the US not acknowledge territories taken by military force.

Henry Lewis Stimson was the next Secretary of State after Secretary Kellogg. He was a Harvard Graduate and Attorney, as well as served as Secretary of War and Secretary of State for a number of Presidents. Aside for the aforementioned matters that Secretary Stinson and President Hoover worked on together, Secretary Stinson also handled additional affairs in Latin America. Not to mention after President Hoover's term in office,

Secretary Stinson was appointed Secretary of War by President Truman and assisted in developing procedure for The Nuremberg Trials, which was the trying of Nazi war criminals post World War II. Secretary Stinson also helped develop and direct affairs surrounding the dropping of the Atomic Bomb.

Franklin D. Roosevelt

President Franklin D. Roosevelt took the office as the 32 President during a challenging time for America. He was a Harvard and Columbia Law school graduate and cousin to former former President Theodore Roosevelt. The 1930's were a time of great depression for America, as the stock market had crashed in 1929 and Unemployment rates rose as high as it ever had rose upward 10 million. Not to mention the onset of World War II was on the rise while President Roosevelt's American Troops were to assist Churchill's Great Britain and Stalin's Soviet Union against Hitler's German forces. While China was also considered an ally, Japan, Italy, and Germany were considered the then "Axis of Evil."

Domestically FDR's plan was the New Deal which gave aide to families through Social Security. Also, gold standard was removed and we inquired debt, this was the impetus that led to some of his Criticism. Nevertheless, he was considered one of the greatest Presidents in the realm with Washington and Lincoln according to scholars. Much like President's Trump and Obama's Stimulus package. Notwithstanding FDR put regulation on utilities, and communication, as Trump worked with Congress to develop Paycheck Protection Loans. Federal guaranteed and forgivable loans for Small Businesses to apply for up to 10 million for rehire of their employees and to aide during the Coronavirus attack that struck the World. Almost like a military state, citizens were required to Quarantine and stay home from work, curfews were implemented and extreme measures of precaution were taken to combat the spread of the deadly virus that was killing elderly, youth and those with weak immunity World Wide. Though this be domestic trivia, and this book about forego policy, It also can be mentioned that he was the only President to hold office for three full terms.

In terms of Foreign policy, aside from matters of World War II. Roosevelt had a step down policy with respect to Latin America and the Bannan Wars. He withdrew troops from Cuba, Haiti, and Panama, changing the policies of American forces protecting Latin American territories. It seems that we have continued to be the protectorate of even certain Middle Eastern Counties, policing their streets in Iraq and Afghanistan and being further drawn into their feuds and infrastructure and had to have our troops withdrawn to allow these countries to man their own streets, and run their own homeland security.

Cordell Hull was the longing serving Secretary of State in U.S. history. As he was appointed by President Roosevelt and severed for the elven years that Roosevelt served in office, he started off as a Senator and a Judge, and had his own aspirations for the Vice Precedency and Oval Office before he was appointed Secretary of State. In terms of Foreign policy, Secretary Hull had took on the "Good Neighbor" policy as he sought to better relations with Latin American Countries in the midst of Roosevelt's Step down of troops. The strategy was that this policy would promote better trade relations amongst Latin American nations instead of inciting resentment.

Secretary Hull main focus was increasing International trade among all nations and foreign powers. Mr. Hull battled high tariffs, as he thought that they led to the depression.

Edward Reilly Stettinius Jr. severed as Secretary of State after Secretary Hull until the terminus of President Roosevelt's and even the inception of President Truman's administration. Essentially Secretary Stettinius was a business man. He held positions with General Motors and the Steel Company before getting into politics. His main contributions during his tenure were that he helped bring the War to a close with President Roosevelt as well as attended the frost United Nations Conference in San Francisco in 1945 where 50 allied nations formed and developed the United Nations under Truman.

Chapter 33

Harry S. Truman

Heavy was the crown that Mr. Truman had to wear when he became the 33rd President. Although he was not a King, because we are not a Monarchy but a capitalistic Democratic Society, the weight and issues of War were immediately upon him and his administration. And, although he was Vice President under Truman, he was little aware of the development of the Atomic Bomb, that he would drop on Hiroshima and Nagasaki. Further, there were Soviet Union Pressures that he would have to manage.

Genius in his administrative abilities President Truman served as a Judge and Senator before his rise to the Presidential office and was said to be responsible for fiscal policies and rooting out corruption and waste saving upward 14 billion dollars. Again, although this book be primarily about Chiefs of state and foreign policy, President Truman mad some progressive additions to the New Deal which was developed under President Roosevelt. He had a 21 bullet point program that he shot off to congress in which Social Security was expanded along with Unemployment, Housing, and the cleaning up of slums.

The Russians were bullying Turkey and guerrilla militias were poised to take over territory in Greece. It's interesting history, because during WWII, the Soviet Under Stalin was pretty much our Allies, but as they blocked Western Berlin, Truman ordered Airlifts of aide to the people. Along with these matters, Truman had Western Unity among Western Nations on his mind, an came up with a strategic military organization that we may not all familiar with, or at least have heard of;--NATO, that is, Northern Atlantic Treaty Organization, founded in 1949.

Next on the Foreign Policy Radar, was the bad acting and behavior of North Korea in attacking His neighbor and brother, South Korea. From reading certain documents, in my assessment, I presume that North Korea was almost decimated with the dropping of another Atomic Bomb. I am not sure what prevented such protective measures. Probably the utter destruction that happen to those cities in Japan and a sense of humanity that did not want to see the after effects of radiation and such loss of civilian life. But such are the casualties of War. After all we could not Bomb the whole world. So, President Truman limited our interaction, as the UN got involved because consequences of our over involvement could have been retaliation from both Russia and China.

James Francis Byrnes was pointed by President Truman as Secretary of State and was an asset to the President's cabinet during the interim and transition period between WWII and the Cold War.

Bayne found himself in a law office being tutored by Chief Justices at the tender age of 7. He eventually would go on to college, law school, and pass the bar in South Carolina. In his career he was elected to the Senate and served there for a decade as well as did private practice and was a key member of President Roosevelt's Economic Security Staff.

Under President Truman's administration, Secretary Baynes travelled extensively. Secretary Baynes was also fortunate enough to travel with the President to the Potsdam Conference in Germany post WWII, where the big three; Stalin, Churchill, and Truman met to reconcile new European borders after German surrender. The first World War was considered as well as the postwar reparation payment that were imposed upon Germany and apparently boggled down their economy. Some sources report that this strategy of imposing payments upon Germany is what catalyzed the rise of the Nazi regime.

There was a divide between the Soviet Union and remaining Ally powers who were ready to sign a treaty for Japan's "utter destruction" if they did not surrender, but due to the fact that the Soviet had yet to declare war on Japan, they refused to sign. These negotiation meetings the Cold War and the three allied powers never met again collectively to discuss Post WWII diplomacy matters.

George C. Marshall was the third Secretary of State who served in President Hoover's cabinet. He attended Military College in Virginia and did served in both WWI and WWII. He gradually arose through success in his career to a five-star general in the US Army and was appointed as the Army Chief of Staff by President Roosevelt. Although he was Secretary of State under President Truman's administration.

As Secretary of State under Truman, Secretary Marshall had the mission to go the China and help negotiate tension between both Communist and patriots in China. His mission failed in mitigating the circumstances in this particular diplomatic bather, but there were others were he was victorious for the interest of the country and his career.

One major development that was attributed to Secretary Marshall was the "Marshall Plan;" this plan was a multi-international stimulus package if you will for Western European countries to help them recover after the Second World War and the prevent the spread of Communism. Countries who received aide were the UK, France, Asia under a separate package, and although the Soviet Union refused this stimulus, as well as interfered in Hungry, Poland ,and Eastern Europe receiving their aide, America was kind and just in her dealings.

The next Secretary of State to serve under President Truman was Dean Acheson. He had a prestigious educational background, attending Yale for undergrad and Harvard for law school. He worked in the private sector for a firm for a time then the state and finally his appointments.

There were many ideological and diplomatic fronts during Secretary Acheson's time as Secretary of State. Actually, He was one to consider the Soviet Union as a possible global threat and power, more than Communistic ideology, but a hindrance to free states globally. He did not want this thinking to influence Germany. China was ultimately lost to Communism and the nationalist sought refuge in Taiwan. Part of the United States interest also included the rebuilding of Japan after both atomic bombs were dropped on their infrastucute and cities of Hiroshima and Nagasaki.

46

Chapter 34

Dwight D. Eisenhower

Dwight D. Eisenhower served as the 34 President of the United States of America;--a time after WWII and during the Cold War. A time when there was negotiations that had to happen between US and Korea as well as matters that needed to be addressed concerning the Soviet Union. President Eisenhower, before he was President, attended college at West Point in Texas, as he was born in Kansas. Some positions he held before his presidency were the Chancellor of Columbia University as well assumed to the highest position of command of NATO forces.

After his time as a NATO Commander he was actually persuaded by his peers to run for President of the United States. He would develop a sort of treaty with Russian while he was in office and it was actually the death of Joseph Stalin that disrupted and changed US-Russia Relations. There were eventually meetings in Geneva with executive leadership from US, Britain, France, and The Soviet. Russia had also developed Hydrogen bombs and it was pertinent topic of discussion during the meeting that US and Russia share information regarding this matter by allowing certain Arial photos to be taken over facilities in both countries. A reach for civility and diplomacy instead of a vicious and deadly theatre of War.

After a near death experience due to a heart attack, President Eisenhower came back to office fighting through segregation laws in his own country. Though this be a book of Foreign relations, it must be noted that domestically Eisenhower was also a silent warrior who sent armed troops to help desegregate Arkansas Schools. Also the whole Armed forces were desegregated under his leadership. He is quoted in one source writing "There is no second-class citizen. In this country."

The first acting Secretary of State for one day was Harrison Freeman Matthews, after Dean Acheson. Mr. Mathews served as an ambassador to three Western Nations and also was Secretary of the Navy during WWI.

The next appointed Secretary of State was John Dulles. He is said to be a global force against communism as well as the terror of the Soviet Union, also promoting coup d'etat in Iran and Guatemala. There was also activity in Viet Cong and Indochina that needed to be considered with respect to France and the spread of communism. He also had a close brother who worked for the Central Intelligence Agency.

As a young man, he was surrounded by diplomats as his grandfather was a past Secretary of State.

He graduated from Preston as well as law school at George Washington University Law and as he was committee appointed he deterred US policy that would hold Germany responsible for reparations cautioning against revolutionary backlash, ie. Nazi uprising.

One treaty that is worth noting is the piece of legislation that restored Japan to full independence under US terms after the Pearl Harbor, and the dropping of the Atomic Bombs toward the climax of WWII. This was a great victory facilitated by Secretary Dulles.

The final Secretary of State under President Eisenhower was Secretary Christian A. Herter who had a number of administrative and executive assistant positions in both the private and government sectors before his time in office. He was a Harvard graduate and the number of activities he assisted with and oversaw in his political career were both far reaching and highly effective. From the time of Roosevelt all the way up to President Lyndon B. Johnson, he played some kind of role if even a voice of dissension. He was elected a statesmen five times.

Diplomatically, Secretary Herter had a lot to manage on his plate. There was the West Berlin Crisis with regards to the Cold war, the shooting down of our U2 Spy plane, early curbing of Fidel Castrol's revolution and it's move toward communism, conflict with Russian and their difficult leader Nikita Khrushchev, and Noise surrounding the Civil war in Congo, Africa.

47

Chapter 35

John F. Kennedy

John F. Kennedy was a Harvard Graduate born in Massachusetts and a WWII Naval Survival and Hero. More accurately, Mr. Kennedy, before he was president, joined the Navy after college and as his ship was attacked by a Japanese destroyer, led his troops to safety upon tempest waters, even though he sustained injury. After the fallout from the war, returning stateside, he married, became a writer, and even won a Pulitzer for his book entitled, *"Profiles in Courage."*

In the oval office, President Kennedy was an aggressor against poverty, and petitioner for civil rights, and legislator for the idea of human rights. He held high the ideals of Peace and Alliance bringing American Genius to the New and developing world in face the obstacle of communism.

Diplomatically, President Kennedy faugh the Soviet's erecting of the Berlin wall by re-enforcing West Berlin troops. Secondly, there was the Cuban situation with Fidel Castro well rooted in his territory, so much so, that even as President Kennedy approved Cuban exiles to return to Cuba for the intention of uprooting and toppling Castro and his regime in the "Bay of Pigs Invasion";--this squeamish was ultimately unsuccessful.

One thing that was effective was President Kennedy's issue of a sort of moratorium against all sea travel and movement of weapons as sly Russia attempted to transport nuclear weapons to Cuba that they may be within range of North American territories. It has been documented Soviet missile bases on Cuban shores was Fidel's idea after a secret meeting between Castro and Soviet leader Nikita Khrushchev as a retaliation to the Bay of Pigs Invasion to prevent future US attacks. Apparently US-military reconnescience U2 Spy Aircraft picked up location of Soviet Missile bases on Cuban shores, Hence the "Cuban Missal Crisis." The world was in terror and on the brink of Global Nuclear War.

Moving forward, President Kennedy through arbitration of the United Nations insisted that Soviet military engineers publically dismantle and remove and further agree not to bring any more High artillery, ie. ballistic missiles or nuclear warheads, to Cuban territories with the intention of North American attack.

Livingston T. Merchant was the first acting Secretary of State under President Kennedy. He had more previous appointments with the department of State and Undersecretary Appointments as he served in various positions in government after Pearl Harbor and at the climax of the Cold War. His time was short in this position under President Kennedy as he was only holding the position.

The next, and official Secretary of State to hold this office in the Kennedy administration was David Dean Rusk. He studied political science in his early undergrad years and completed a Masters then went on to teach in academia while and ultimately attending law school and University of California, Berkley.'

Eventually Rusk would join the Army and be inducted into the Military Intelligence Branch of the War Department. He climbed in rank, and served in a number of positions in the War Department before his discharge and sitting on the committee of International Security Affairs as well as one on Special Political Affairs.

Secretary Rusk had his onn ideals about the way foreign policy should be done although he also supported President Kennedy in his decision making. Mr. Rusk saw the underdeveloped nations around the world as an opportunity for US philanthropy through humanitarian and technological aide. He wanted US relations to give underdeveloped countries the tools they needed to progress into the twentieth century. Secretory Rusk favored diplomatic means and arbitration when dealing with Russia and keeping the lines of communication open.

48

Chapter 36

Lyndon B. Johnson

Lyndon B. Johnson was born in Texas and knew poverty from a personal his own childhood experiences. He grew strong and became a High school teacher by profession, and before ascending to the Vice Presidency under Kennedy, and the President after the Kennedy assassination he also served in the House and Senate for a number of years, taking on leadership roles also in that arena.

Mr. L.B. Johnson also served for a time in the Navy as a lieutenantcommander during WWI. And amongst his domestic programs in his Presidency was his War on Poverty, Civil Rights, New Deal, Social Security, and Healthcare, to name a few items he majored on. With respect to Foreign policy, there was the draft and stopping communism Vietnam with the war. As we know, the late 60's were a heated time in American history with respects to civil rights, the Vietnam war, Assignations, Black Leaders, and overall civil unrest.

Interstellar astronauts orbited the moon during President Johnson's administration. And his idea was to create a "Great Society." In this society, in President's heart he wanted peace and was continually confronted with the communist Vietnam threat and War plus riotous commotion at home stateside primarily in the Black community despite his efforts for civil rights. I've often wondered to myself, being born in '80, and I hope this does not sound insensitive to my Vietnam friends, but why did we not drop another atomic bomb like we did with Japan, to win the war in spite of all the military casualties that we took.

Of course, I don't know all the behind the scene politics, weight of the Oval Office, and the inner dealings a President has to think through when considering the complexities of International War and Peace, but it seemed like a simple, and quick fast solution to the problem at the time. But how would that decisive decision had affected the world, and how America would have been viewed as a nation that would literally obliterate any nation or people who faced us in military challenge. Perhaps this is why President Johnson refused to run for a second term, or maybe there were other personal matters that he considered. Nevertheless, he is held in esteem as a great President.

David Rusk who also served with President Kennedy and after his death with President Johnson, kept persistent with Vietnam War policies. On such treaty of pact that was formed in order to protect against the spread communism that existed in

North Vietnam was SAETO—which stood for South East Asian Treaty Agreement. It was a pact between the United States, France, Great Britain, New Zealand, Australia, the Philippines, Thailand and Pakistan. Each nation had its own political, militarily, and economic reasons for being apart of this treaty or organization, but overall it promoted a sort of blockade to stop communism, legal means for continued infiltration of North Vietnam, as diplomats and military remained in the region, and other international interests being met. Also, it must be noted that that certain nations such as Vietnam, Cambodia, and Laos, weren't allowed to ally with or join any other international military organization per 1954 discussions at the Geneva Convection.

49

Chapter 37

Richard Nixon

Richard Nixon as president had huge successes as well as major defeats. He brought the Vietnam War to a close, mitigated relations between the Soviet Union and China, and also Nixon was born in California and attended Whittier College an Duke law school. He also had a stint in the Navy as a Lieutenant Commander serving in the Pacific like President Kennedy. He held the office of Representative and Senator in California—all roles he served in before ascending to the Presidency.

Domestically Nixon held conservative values, promoting revenue sharing in cooperation, not to be confused with communism, the end of the draft, new anticrime laws, and broad environmental development programs. There was also the landing on the moon of Apollo 11.

Internationally, as aforementioned, there was the de-escalation and pull out of Vietnam. Many of these matters were tactfully negotiated by Secretary of State Henry Kissinger, for example the Yom kipper War in Israel Also carefully cultured relations between Soviet leader Leonid I. Brezhnev and Nixon to limit Nuclear war strategy.

At the early terminus of the Nixon Presidency which ended in his resignation, due to suspect and illegal activity of certain individuals breaking into the Democratic Campaign office;--namely the infamous "Watergate Scandal."

Charles E. Bohlen was the first acting Secretary of State in the Nixon administration. He was a graduate of Harvard College and had a long diplomatic history going back to his assisting President Roosevelt and Harry Hopkins during WWII diplomatic trips back and forth to Moscow. Considered a Soviet expert, he served in some capacity or the other for the state department in Eisenhower, Kennedy, and Johnson's administration. Ironically, although he was considered a Soviet expert unlike Condoleezza Rice, whom we will discuss later, a Russian expert in her own right;-- he was demoted from his Ambassadorship by President Eisenhower because his relations with Soviet leadership and the US Secretary of State Dulles les at the time were not negotiable, or conflictual at best. Serving only as acting Secretary in the Nixon administration after a long career, William P. Rogers was the next and first official Secretary of State in President Nixon's cabinet.

William P. Rogers also held a number of positions before his appointment to the office of Secretary of State. He was a Cornell University of Law School graduate and shortly thereafter a Lieutenant

Commander in the US Navy. Following his time in military service he sat on a number of congressional Subcommittees looking into matters of the Department of Defense, and moreover, served as an Attorney General during President Eisenhower's time in the office

In his office, Secretary Rogers was instrumental in bringing temporary peace in the Middle East and also was one of the signers of the Vietnamese Peace treaty. Not to mention his technological genius in pulling for massive renovation in the State Department's filing system, introducing advanced technology and computer systems in government offices for managing the overwhelming amount of paperwork and other necessary computational programs.

One other issue that Secretary Rogers is famously known for, although it was not as successful as he would have liked it to be, was his push for Arab-Israeli peace between one another and his drawing up his coined "Roger's Plan" that brought UN world powers together to enforce or stop the two brother nations from constantly fighting and waring with one another. Unfortunately, proper terms could not be agreed upon for the UN nations to properly oversee and contain such conflict. Those nations called to action were, The USA, UK, Soviet Union, and France.

After his tenure, Secretary Rogers continue to sit on certain UN committees that dealt with matters of

Southwest Arica, as well as continued to work at his law practice in the private sector.

The next acting Secretary of State was Kenneth Rush. He was born in Washington and end up attending Duke University where he was collegiate acquaintances with the then young and ambitious Richard Nixon. Mr. Rush graduated from Law School and became a Assistant Professor where he taught Law to college students. He was actually appointed Deputy Secretary by Richard Nixon and before this in his position of Ambassador to Germany; he was extremely instrumental in negotiating East-West Berlin relations as he rigorously worked at his task for some 17 months. Further, the good that came from this deal was that the four nations US, UK, Soviet Union, and France ended tensions and settled matters with respect to Berlin. This deal also eased matters between US=Soviet relations.

Next up to bat holding the office of Secretary of State officially was the O So famous and Great Henry Kissinger. I've always heard his name mentioned, but never really knew or understood his role in politics or what he was so well known for. Well, I learned that he was a Jewish refugee who fled Nazi Germany with his family in 1938. Further he was awarded the Nobel Peace prize under controversial circumstances. He served as Secretary of State, as well as National Security Advisor;--instrumental to the cessation of bullets flying in Vietnam.

In terms of education and career, Kissinger was a Harvard Ph.D. Graduate and worked as faculty in the Government and International Affairs department. Before that, He was a Germen interpreter for the Army during WWII. Selected by Nixon to be His National Security Advisor, he also concurrently served as Secretary of State.

Further notes in foreign policy on Secretary Kissinger, he was responsible to the end of the Yon Kippur War, opened engagement with China, and had skin in the game in Argentina, not to mention supported Pakistan during Bangladesh War in spite of the genocide present in that region. Ironically former Secretary Kissinger is held as a War Criminal by some journalist and lawyers, but this does not take away from his prolific writing career of some 12 books on Foreign policy and geopolitical history.

Chapter 38

Gerald Ford

Vice President Gerald Ford took the Oval Office upon the resignation of President Richard Nixon behind the "Watergate Scandal." Shortly thereafter, he was officially inaugurated and took on the challenge of a nation suffering from inflation, on the brink of a recession, energy shortages, and having to keep up a stable foreign policy measure throughout the New World. Mr. Ford was born in Nebraska, and spent his young adult years at the University of Michigan. He played football in college and went to Yale to assistant Coach and there graduated from Law school. He joined the Navy Reserves like many other past Presidents, meriting the rank of lieutenant commander during WWII.

In terms of international relations, Vietnam collapsed some three quarters of the year after President Ford took office, so US ambition and interaction in that realm was no longer so much of a headache. Other matters around the globe at that time, such as US-Soviet relations were eased by the Détente accords. Much like arbitration, or negotiations, communication alleviated tension between the two nuclear powers as the Cold War was coming to an end. Also, involved in these Détente talks was China, as Ford made is Far East visit as a show of US solidarity.

Further on the Soviet Union, were the Helsinki Watch, which performed much like a third party watch dog inspecting facilities to make sure there were no compliance issues. This independent private agency functioned much like the modern day UN inspecting nuclear facilities in Iran to make sure of uranium levels and nuclear proliferation is curbed.

Secretary Henry Kissinger stayed on staff after the resignation of President Richard Nixon due to "Watergate Scandal." It is sited that he aided President Ford in getting acquainted with the International Scene of Affairs and together they continued much of President Nixon's Foreign Policy agenda;--especially with respect to the Détente accords with Soviet Russia, engaging China, and further talks in the Middle East.

52

Chapter 39

James "Jimmy" E. Carter

Mr. Jimmy Carter served as the thirty-ninth President of the United States of America. Often famously known for his Peanut business as well as his peace deals brokered between Israel and Egypt, President Carter was and is much more. Having written over some 30 books, some political and otherwise, he was a Naval Academy graduate and joined the Navy as an Officer, he served on submarines. After the news of his Businessman father's death, decided to discharge from the Navy, settle matters at home, and become an entrepreneur in the family peanut business. I always heard that he was also a Great Sunday School teacher and when he introduced himself it was with a small sample of his farms peanuts.

Although President Carter a huge social President in his domestic affairs, aiding civil rights, social security, energy matters, and even rights for African-Americans and Women, this is not a book of domestic social policy, but of International affairs and Foreign policy. In this vein, when President Carter took his human rights attitude oversees too to greet the Soviet Union, he was met with a cold shoulder at first. Notwithstanding, he ultimately made progress with the aforementioned SALT II nuclear limitation treaty. I guess this would be the Cold War equivalent to Trump's modern day denuclearization talks with Kim Jon Un and North Korea.

Further things that mirror modern day international politics was President Carter's initiation of full diplomatic relations with China Treaty. We know that Trump recently signed trade agreements with China lifting some Tariffs and opening up many markets especially in the Agriculture Sector, more specifically--Corn. This does fly in the face of the recent espionage attacks that some high level University and pharmaceutical characters are being charged in the States for. Not to mention the recent COVID-19 scare originating from China.

Traumatic events worth mentioning were the Soviet's Invasion of Afghanistan, and 52 American's being held hostage by Iran. President's Carter's negotiation tactics seemed futile and falling upon Iran's deaf ears as the American Hostages were finally released upon the US new election cycle and President Carter leaving office.

In terms of secretaries of state whom served during President Carter's administration, there were three acting who held the office in a matter of a month in the same year and two official,-- that is, Cyrus Vance and Edmund Muske. The other three before these two, with the exception of Philip Habib actually substituted twice for the position under President Carter.

Phillip Habib attended the University of Idaho for Forestry, and then went on to attain a Ph.D. from Berkley in the same subject matter. He was actually recruited for his diplomatic career after testing within in the ranks of the top 10% for Foreign Affairs. Considered an intellectual and one of the foremost political diplomats, he held a number of special envoy positions for President Regan to the Middle East and East Asia. Only serving as acting deputy Under Secretary of State of Political affairs for a short time in President Carter's cabinet, he fulfilled other foreign affair roles with distinction, discipline and dedication. Roles such as, aiding in the diplomatic neutralizing of the Israeli-Syria and Israeli-PLO conflict in 1891,again during Regan's administration. Mr. Habib also served in the Army during WWII and achieved the rank of Captain.

Cy Vance was the first official Secretary of State in the Carter administration. He attended Yale for his Bachelor's degree as well as for Law School, and after some years in the private sector joined the ranks of the expert government workers and eventually found himself contracted with the Department of Defense. Under President Lyndon B. Johnson, Mr. Vance was selected to be the Deputy of Defense and originally wholeheartedly supported the War in Vietnam, but then adamantly opposed it, lobbying for President Johnson to return troops stateside.

Secretary Vance's Foreign Policy philosophy was diplomatic over malarial. He used policy to continue the limitation of Weaponry in Soviet Union and also negotiated peace deals between isreal and Arab nations. He released American controls with regards to the Panamc Canal and further reengaged trade relations with China. Finally Secretary Vance made a push for quasi sort of democratic state in Zimbabwe, where the majority ruled.

One major issue where Secretary Vance and President Carter had conflict on was the President's resolve on what to do with regards to Iran and the establishing of the Islamic Republic, not to mention militia students capturing some 52 American hostages in a US Embassy. Secretary Vance felt that some of President's Carters ideals on what to do were and would be disruptive to his continued negotiation tactics, and therefore resigned before President Carter finished his term. As mentioned above, the American hostages were released unharmed upon the completion of President Carter's time in office.

Warren Christopher had a sagacious political career emanating from his graduating from Stanford Law School and serving as Deputy Attorney General in President LBJ's administration. He was Deputy Secretary of State under President Carter's administration and held the office of Secretary of Stare only for a short time as he was a sort of sub, but as we will discuss later, he also held the official position in President Clinton's administration, implemented effective foreign policies, and was a

Professor at UCLA in his years after serving in the Presidential cabinet.

David D. Newsom was the following "acting" Secretary of State after Mr. Warren Christopher. He held a number of Ambassador positions; that is, to Libya, Africa, Indonesia, and the Philippines. He was also a writer for the Christian Science Monitor publishing over five books.

Edmund Muskie was the last Secretary of State to serve alongside President Carter. He as many of his predecessors had a history of political involvement, ranging from House and Senate congressman to Governorship in Main, to the office of the Vice Presidency, to Runner up for the Oval Office before he was selected by President Carter to serve as Secretary of State. Apparently, Secretary Muskie was selected after the resignation of Secretary Vance for reasons of the death of 8 servicemen in the administrations attempted mission to rescue American Hostages from the grasp of Iranian. Terrorists in what was then known as "Operation Eagle Claw." Further details on this mission; --Airforce and Marine Aircraft flew launching from Naval Aircraft Carriers, to Iranian territory and landed in football fields to carry on mission. Six months of continuous flying happen for preparation for this moment. This was a time when there was no stealth technology. Delta and Ranger Special Forces were upon the carrier aircraft. CIA had went before to help coordinate landing of the Aircraft. More than six never flown before helicopters were launched to the desert of Iran to help carry out the assault, flying at an altitude of 5,000ft.

Mr. Edmund Muskie was a graduate of Cornell University Law School and sort of a local hero as he served in Main and on a number of Foreign Relation Committee's in the Senate. Not to mention his Naval Service as he enlisted during WWII and took to sea. Secretary Muskie also helped develop and implement the Carter Doctrine which further limited Soviet preventing movement into the Middle East and the Gulf of Persia.

Ronald Regan

Mr. Ronald Wilson Regan was the fortieth President of the United States of America. He attended Eureka College and was born in Illinois. Majoring in Economics and Sociology, which would later help assist in his economic plan and policies as President, he also played football and did drama in college. Picked up by Screening, took on an acting career and performed in just under 60 movies.

Throughout Regan's Hollywood career, he was elected President of the Actors Guild and although he was a liberal in college, was personally challenged and conflicted over the rampant communism depicted in the film industry. He took a stand and became conservative and even a spokesmen for conservatism, as a TV host and traveled the country. As He would eventually run for the Oval Office, he won in a landslide victory, as Americans were said fatigued from the yearlong hostage situation in Iran and wanted a change from President Jimmy Carter.

As aforesaid, President Regan's background in economics led him to develop policies that fought inflation, unemployment, stimulated the economy and also allocated certain funds toward the Department of Defense. So much so, was President Regan committed to his economic plan and policies that despite tax cuts, and increased national deficits, he refused to turn or back down from his continued support of funds to national defense.

With respect to International Relations-President Regan had a "Peace through Strength" ideology. This would explain his ramp in Department of Defense and spending and support. Further, he negotiated with then Soviet Prime Minister Mikhail Gorbachevto to do away with mid-range nuclear missiles. Moreover, he also hit by bombing Lybia for their association with the attack on US Combat Soldiers in West Berlin.

One unfortunate event was that happen during the time of President Regan's first term in office was the suicide truck bombing of US barracks in Beirut. There was Civil War going on amongst the Lebanese and US along with multinational peace keeping troops were sent to keep order. A fully loaded Truck bomber hit our barracks. At this sudden news, President Regan withdrew the surviving Marine ground troops and performed airstrikes on Syrian targets in Lebanon from a Navy Battleship.

On an upside, President Regan won in his decision to invade Grenada. It's what is known as "Operation Urgent Fury," and US troops, that is Marines, Army, Delta Force, and Navy SEALS went into the Caribbean territory to disrupt the ill-aligned Marxist-Leninist government and protect some medical students that were said to be in danger from the subtle growing Russian militia that was spreading in the region. In the aftermath, a new leader was put in position, and democratic elections were held. US troops completed the mission in a number of days and then withdrew from the territory. This response was all at the request from the Organization of Eastern Caribbean States in a plea for HELP. Their Prime Minister Maurice Bishop was demonstrating a strange form of tyranny in imprisoning certain political leaders that posed threat to his ideals and office.

The first Secretary of State to serve in the Regan Administration had a long and developed military and government service career history. He was none other than, Alexander Haig and He attended and graduated from West Point Military Academy and went on to graduate from Georgetown. Further, He served in both the Korean and Vietnam War. Not to mention he served as adviser to Henry Kissinger as well as held a number of Deputy Secretary Positions to past Presidents as well as held the office of National Security Advisor before being appointed to Secretary of State by President Regan

Secretary Haig wanted to give the office of Secretary of State a new look as well as strengthen the position in comparison to his past predecessors. One could understand his desire given his intense military history and background. During his term, there were several fronts of battle that he took on. There was there was the Soviet pressure in Afghanistan, Dealings with trade in

China as well as Taiwan, Poland, Britain and Argentina, and the slowly rising conflict between Israel, Syria and Lebanon.

Apparently, Secretary Haig had to perform an extremely careful diplomatic procedure in renegotiating relations with China while continuing to allow arms to be sold to Taiwan. He also had success in re-directing NATO agenda to benefit US interest. His besetting area was that of the Middle East and is said to ultimately have led to his resignation among other inner political dealings within the Regan Cabinet with respect to Foreign policy.

The acting Secretary of State in the interim after Secretary Haig was Walter J. Stoessel Jr. He only held the position for a short time before George P. Shultz took office, but he had a long and rewarded professional career in government. He serve as Ambassador to a number of nations, Including Poland, and Germany. Not to mention he was also the US Ambassador to the Soviet Union for a time. Graduating from Stanford and then pursuing graduate studies at Columbian University, all to embark upon the nation as an international civil leader and servant who brought intellectual and military aide and leadership to the committees, boards, and cabinets he sat upon. For these things he was awarded The Distinguished Diplomatic Metal of Honor.

George Shultz majored in Economics at Princeton University and while serving in the Marine Corps

Reserves after his discharge he earned his Ph.D. from MIT in the subject matter of industrial economics. He held a number of positions in government in the Department of Labor and serving in the Treasury Department putting his economics degree to good use before being appointed to the position of Secretary of State by President Ronald Regan.

Like many who came into the ranks of high government office, or any executive position for that matter, Secretary Shultz was left a small stack of Foreign policy matters of decision that he would have to determine in which way to proceed. There was war in Lebanon, and dealings with the People Republic of China as well as negotiations with the principal officers in Taiwan. Not to mention, there sudden and ongoing flare ups of the Cold War with a temperamental Soviet Union.

55

George H. W. Bush

George Herbert Walker Bush was the forty-fist President of the United States of America. He was born in Massachusetts and after attending Phillips Academy decided to join the military, more specifically he was trained as a Naval Pilot Bomber and flew just under 60 missions. In the Pacific theater during WWII he was shot down by antiaircraft artillery by the Japanese and rescued by US submarines. Considered a War Hero, he received the Distinguished Flying Cross, a high ranking award given to those who distinguished themselves in combat aerial missions.

Mr. Bush was occupied with completing his education after his Naval Career, and attended Yale University, where after graduation he took an intrigue to politics and public service. After serving and a Council member in the House of Representatives in Texas, he was selected for a number of key level positions within the United States Government. He sat on committee to the People Republic of China, served as an Ambassador to the UN, as well as the Director of the Central

Intelligence Agency, not to mention serving as Vice President to President Regan.

As President, Bush saw the world change dramatically. Internationally speaking, he was witness to the berlin wall coming down, Communist Regimes break apart, Soviet powers The threat of Soviet powers became impotent, The freedom and reign of democracy was making Alexandrian hedge way throughout the world. President Bush Senior brought Panamanian drug lords to justice and sent American Troops to that region of South America to guard and protect the security of the canal which was threatened by excessive drug trafficking.

President Bush also joined at the impetus that which would be the Longest ongoing War in American History. Iraq's leader Saddam Husain invaded Kuwait and made advances toward Saudi Arabia. US and Allied forces countered and retaliated with ground troops as well as Superior Air Power. Operation Desert Storm was embarked upon as our Armed Forces fought in the desert with Courage, Bravery and American Pride.

The Frist Secretary of State to serve in President Bush's administration was only substitute for a short time. It was non-other than Michael Armacost who is currently alive and a fellow at Stanford and also served as president to the Brookings Institute for seven years. Both of these out-fits are research Think Tank oriented organizations focused on International policies, Promoting democracy, and the Rule of Law among other activities. He served in the office of Secretary of State for only five days.

The next Secretary up was James Baker. He had a very involved political and legal career with a few of the American Presidents. After attending a special magnet school for politics, he went on to graduate from Princeton and even served in the United States Marine Corps. Graduated from law school in Texas and took jobs with the state department in government affairs. Namely, various positions in Nixon and Regan administration, He served Chief of staff a few times and served in the department of Commerce along with President Ford. His last position to serve along with a President was Chief of Staff in the cabinet of President H.W. Bush Yet he continues to extend his political acumen through being involved in various Think Tank organizations that focus on Foreign policy.

Diplomatically, Secretary Baker saw the ending of communism and the Cold War. He tried to expeditiously implement his "Baker Plan" which would have reallocated Japanese surplus to other problem areas throughout the world, which were matters of Third World Debt. Being a Military Veteran, as well as holding chief positions in the State Department, then Secretary Baker ensured an Alliance of nations to help resist Saddam Hussain and stop further Iraqi penetration into Kuwait during what was known as the "Persian Gulf War."

Finally, Secretary Baker showed grave interest in smarting the Palestinian-Israeli conflict. One of his policies were to deny any and all funding and recognition to the Palestinian Liberation Organization (PLO) whether directly or indirectly, thus US funding sources were cut even to the UN. Further, he was present during the Madrid Conference of 1991 giving impetus to all present Arab-Israeli nations to stop their infighting and resolve their problems.

The final Secretary of State in the H.W. Bush Administration was none other than Lawrence Sidney Eagleburger. He was born a resident of Wisconsin and there earned his Bachelor's degree from the local University. He went on to serve as Lieutenant in the US. Army and from there came back to get his Master's. He had a number of analytical positons within the state department. His areas of focus were Cuba, Yugoslavia,--more specifically the economic department of the US Embassy there. He served on National Security Council boards as assistant Secretary as well as was within range to the Secretary of State position years before he actually was appointed as he also served as an aide to the Under Secretary of State during the President Kennedy's and Johnson's administration.

Secretary Eagleburger also held political positions for the state department under President Nixon's and Carter's administration. All such analytical and leadership positions evidently were preparation for his tenure as Secretary of State in the Cabinet of President H.W. Bush. Much like Secretary Condoleezza' Rice's preparation in Russian Studies prepared her for diplomacy with Russian President Putin during the Bush Administration, likewise Secretary Eagleburger's analytical positions on Yugoslavia prepared him for dealings with Yugoslavia during H.W. Bush's time in office. Controversial to say the least, Secretary Eagleburger served as adviser on Yugoslavian affairs and politically landed on the side of Serbia dismissing any war crimes or atrocities committed in Croatia. Secretary Eagleburger also had involvement with the Persian Gulf War along with President Bush and continued to work on International problems in an Iraqi study group after his time in office

56

Chapter 42

William "Bill" J. Clinton

The forty-second President of the United States of America was none other than the guy with the silver tongue, Bill Clinton. Otherwise being known as a great Speaker, Economist, Foreign Policy Strategist, and someone who could talk his way through any land mined filled terrain, Clinton was one of the Presidents I remember of my generation as I was in High School during his tenure. I remember and honestly, I feel a little guilty because his autobiography has been sitting in my collection for some time now, and I really want to read it, but somehow have not made my way through it just yet. This year Bill, This year! Anyway, before I get started on his education and political acumen; I remember how we use to joke in High school about how the President said He smoked weed but never "inhaled." I myself wasn't a weed smoker, but always thought that was a pretty funny response. I really shouldn't say this, especially before the business of what we are getting to, but now as an adult, it also seems really funny. The scandle, where a young pretty intern was "supposedly" shining off our President in the Oval office to the point that seaman was found on her dress. Maybe I don't have all the facts straight, but it makes me laugh.

Alright, I hope that doesn't get me into any trouble, High School memories. Anyway, aside from these few Piccadilly's, which were amplified simply because of the position, President Clinton as I remember was held in great esteem, especially in the African-American Community. Sources say, he was the first Democratic President since Roosevelt, balanced the budget to the point of surplus, and experienced all time low unemployment and inflation during his term. As well as increased homeownership all throughout the country. President Clinton led on a platform of wanting to end racial discrimination. I can remember one of my friend's Father, every week I would go to my Buddy's house, and he would be telling me how there is something about this President Clinton, he keeps appointing African Americans to important positions in government. These are some of the good things I remember about President Clinton.

President Clinton was born in Arkansas, and went on to graduate from Georgetown University in his undergrad years. He merited a Rhode Scholar Scholarship to Oxford, and completed his Law Degree at Yale. Thus started his political career, and somewhere around there met his superwomen Wife, Hillary who was a major advocate for children and families in those days, and whom would eventually go on to run for the Presidency herself, and also serve as Secretary of State in the Obama Administration.

In terms of Foreign Policy, which is the focus of this book, President Clinton came to the aide of war torn Bosnia by deploying Peace keeping Troops. He also shocked the nation as we sat watching "Bombs over Bagdad" (Outkast, 2000), or our airstrikes against Iraq due to Saddam Hussain's stubborn incredulity, would not allow him to accept the fact that if he did not comply with the necessary inspections to determine if he was harvesting or building chemical, nuclear, and biological weapons; there would be severe and detrimental consequences released upon his nation. I remember very distinctly watching the television screen and seeing multiple shining's lights and flares going through the dark night as camera or some journalist recorded our missiles striking our enemy at the time with extreme force and power.

Of course, there were many other actions taken in terms of International Relations during President Clinton's administration; I will not go into detail for every such act of war or diplomacy. There was the tragedy in Mogadishu, Civil War in Rwanda, The settlement paid to Iran, because of an Iranian commercial airliner we shot down, the signing of US-China trade relations, and yet the "accidental bombing" of a Chinese Embassy, and finally the meeting at camp David between Israeli and Palestinian leaders Ehud Barak and Yasser Arafat along with President Clinton where terms of peace between Israel and Palestine were not then attained.

President Clinton was also known to be hard on drug trafficking and was admired in all countries as he travelled the world; Europe, Africa, Russia, China, and South America;--as other nations sought the freedom and prosperity of our great country.

Arnold Lee Kanter was the first acting Secretary of State to serve during President Clinton's administration. Prior to this he was Undersecretary of State for 2 years. He also served in a teaching capacity at two Universities==namely University of Ohio and Michigan. Other prior occupations were Research and Analyst work in the government contract and Private sector.

The second acting Secretary of State in President Clinton's cabinet was Frank George Wisner II. His father served in the CIA just under 55 years. He was sent as special envoy to Egypt by President Barak Obama to help mitigate tension between protestors and certain government leaders. Among other nations in which he served as an Ambassador were Zambia, India, and the Philippines'.

The first official Secretary of State to take the office in President Clinton's administration was Warren Christopher. He served in a number of secretarial and judicial positions during his political ascensions; including started out as a clerk for a judge. He also served as Attorney General under President Johnson and Deputy Secretary of State for President Carter.

In terms of diplomacy and International relations, Secretary Christopher tasked himself with enlarging the number of allied members within NATO (North Atlantic Treaty Organization.). Also, challenging China with respect to Human Rights and also seeing to the ending of the Bosnian War through Treaty. Secretary Christopher along with President Clinton also had his hand on attempting to bring Israel and Palestine together for Peace.

The next Secretary of State appointed by President Clinton was a Women of Yugoslavian descent by the name of Madeleine Korbel Albright. Descendent from an immigrant father who was heavily involved in politics and an Ambassador himself, Madeline earned her Bachelor's degree in Political Science with high honors and Graduated with a Ph.D. in Public Law and Government from Columbia University.

She served in the position of Secretary of State for four years in the Clinton administration, but prior to this office she served in number of research, analyst and staff position in the Carter and Clinton Administrations; notwithstanding, she also served an Ambassadorship to the UN. Secretary Albright continued Secretary Christorper's expansion of NATO forces of allied nations, but more specifically into Eastern Europe and she also deterred nuclear proliferation in the Soviet Union along with deploying troops to the aide of Kosovo. It must be noted that Secretary Madeleine Albright was the first women to serve in this capacity in the United

States Government High Office of Secretary of State.

57

58

George W. Bush

President Bush had an arduous task of being a Wartime President at the inception of his incumbency. Months after his swearing in the infamous Terrorist Attack struck our World Trade Center and Pentagon and made aim for the White House by Air Attack through terrorist high jacked American commercial aircraft. Some 3,000 American Citizens lost their lives in the devastation on September 11, 2001. I remember the moment vividly; I was in my apartment in San Diego, California, my 3rd year in College at UCSD. I hadn't left for class yet, and got a call from one of my Frat brother's to turn on the TV. It was unbelievable to see the towers burning with smoke and see images of replay of the jetliners striking them at full speed. The moral on campus was despondent, tense, fearful, anger, sadness, and disbelief. I remember asking one Arabic classmate who happen to be Muslim what they made of everything and they became extremely defensive and suggested that I made them out to be a Terrorist or something. It was strange, but I guess I understood.

Immediately President Bush retaliated with full military Force and disrupted the Taliban along with invading Iraq and toppling Sudden Hussain. Osama bin Laden would be brought to justice through the brutal force of SEAL TEAM 6 under the administration of President Barak Obama, notwithstanding, the never ending war between American soldiers countering insurgents in far off Middle Eastern lands had started. Too many lives maimed or lost to IED's (improvised explosive device) planted by the insurgency as our troops patrolled, protected, fought and took over dangerous territory in Iraq, Afghanistan, and in the many battles fought in the other Middle Eastern countries infected with entrenched Terrorist cells funded, trained, and deployed by the Taliban and Al-Qaeda networks.

President Bush enacted new Homeland Security Laws like the USA Patriot Act in which phone, email, financial and business records could be investigated by the Federal Bureau of Investigation without Warrant in suspicion and to disrupt and intercept any acts of Teresita activity. These efforts were met with some resistance from dissenters as an invasion of privacy, but in my mind, I thought it best served the cause. and if if there were no malicious plots to hide, then American citizens had nothing to worry about.

George Bush graduated from Yale and Harvard with a Business concentration. After his graduation he moved back to Texas to help his Father in the oil Business. Massive income was to be to be made.as

President Bush was to go on and defeat his democratic opponents in two Presidential election campaigns. Not to mention, I believe he was also the governor of Texas.

More specifically on President Bush's Foreign Policy program. He felt that strong economic ties with Latin America was necessary. He believed in Nation Building, providing entry of China into World Trade, and took a strong military defensive position in Missile Defense. I can't be sure, but I think I can remember hearing something to the tune of global democracy in one of his speeches; or democratizing the nations, I could be wrong, but what a concept in juxtaposition to the New World Order agenda.

President Bush was known to reprehend Kim Jong il of North Korea for his development of nuclear, chemical, and biological weapons. Bush thought it a bad idea for the most dangerous weapons to be in the hands of a dangerous nation. Curious that even today under Kim Jung Un's rule; socialist North Korea pulls out of de-n nuclearization deals as well as has aspirations of testing Super Weapons.

In terms of what was going on with Syria, President Bush called for Sanctions on all US accounts to stifle the Science and Technology developmental sector and further prevent Syria from producing weapons of mass destruction. Other foreign policy measures was the enactment of The Syria Accountability and Lebanese Sovereignty Restoration Act (SALSRA) a bill or policy which aimed at ending what US indicated would be Syrian support for Terrorism, and ultimately remove Syrian presence from Lebanon. This happened after the Lebanese Civil War and US also wanted to stop illegal shipment of oil and arms to Un-American terrorist groups in Iraq.

The first Secretary of State to serve in President Bush's administration was a Jamaican from New York by the name of Collen Powel. How do I know this, several years ago I read his book, one of them anyway. And the funny thing is, all I can remember from that massive biography was that his heritage is Jamaican, he joined this ROTC group called the Parsing Rifles as a young man, watched some porn and read a lot of novels. Go figure, I guess you remember the things that resonate with you or that you can relate to. Of course, there was a lot of other political acumen and history during his time in the Bush Cabinet according to his report; like his daily comings and goings in the White house, interaction with other cabinet staff, and the fact that some suggested he run for the Presidency himself, but I don't recall it all so clearly.

I do remember when he was conducting War Strategy meetings on television for the President, or when the media would show clips of how he was adamant about US armed forces being sent overseas with a clear execution and exit strategy for Iraq as to not repeat the mistakes of Vietnam. Ok, that's my freestyle and what I remember without looking at any source, onto the official write up and all the Foreign policy stuff.

Upon reading additional material, it seems that Secretary Powell served as a Deputy Security Advisor for Ronald Regan, a little fact I did not know, and also spent time in Germany, South Korea, and Vietnam. President H.W. Bush appointed Secretary Powell as chairman of the Joint-Chief of Staff. Of course, Secretary Powel was a High Ranking military General in the Army, which goes without saying, and merited his outstanding career through years of service and commitment getting the job done. He was key in leading war strategy in Operation Desert Storm and according to reports, oversaw just under 30 military crisis's during his time in office.

Secretary Powell was a well-rounded Diplomat. He sought to promote diplomacy instead of war when able to do so; he sought sanctions in Iraq, to further increase the pressure and promoted our national missile defense system, On the domestic side of things, he looked after personnel and various departments in State department with funds for improvement.

In terms of the September Terrorist attack, Secretary Powell took decisive and immediate action singling in on Al=Qaeda and demanded cooperation from Afghanistan and Pakistan as to force them to choose a side, and not have any affiliation or be "supporters or harbors" of those committing such heinous acts. Secretary Powell was responsible in obtaining intelligence about Iraq having the capability of manufacturing weapons of mass destruction. He advocated UN inspection, a flashback form history during the Cold War, and presented his intelligence to the UN so that allies would be on board. As aforementioned, he wanted a clear path to execution and exit.

Along with managing war efforts in Afghanistan and Iraq, Secretary Powell had to also consider US dealings with Russian the ever so developing China. The same old fights that President Trump fights today, were fought and won then. Nuclear proliferation in North Korea and Iran were subsided and Lybia stopped its nuclear program all together; a big win. Secretary Powell was also a strong advocate for international funds of support to target against the global aids epidemic.

There were other Foreign issues that Secretary Powell helped manage such as the Tsunami in India, ongoing and almost a nuclear conflict between India and Pakistan, and constant turmoil in the Middle East that Powell felt arose from the old and Ancient Israeli- Palestine conflict in which he was a supporter of an independent Palestinian state; nevertheless no one in Presidents cabinet wanted to enforce such a "Road Map." Finally, Secretary Powell also had something to do with ending the civil conflicts in Liberia and Haiti.

Next up was Secretary Condoleezza Rice. Interestingly enough after reading two of her books because of a dream I had years ago, the only things I remember of her were that her Father was an Alpha, the same fraternity that I pledged in college, that she went to Stanford, knew the four little girls that were killed in the Birmingham church bombing, Spoke fluent Russian, attained her Ph.D. and taught like Russian politics or something of that matter in the ivy league realm of Stanford. Oh yes, and that she also was also in a Sorority and a stanch Christian Republican, her Dad being a minister and all. Of course in her book, she also spoke to the politics of being in the Bush administration and diplomatic conversations with Vladimir Putin as she travelled to Russia and abroad on state business. Ok, that's all I remember, really.

As Collen Powell, was the first African-American male to hold the position of Secretary of State, Condoleezza was the first African-American women to hold the position. Both pioneers of their time, Condoleezza Rice graduated with a Bachelor's degree in Political Science, then went on to graduate school to earn her Master's at the University of Norte Dame, also in Political Science, and then on to the Graduate school of International Studies in Denver, to finish her Ph.D. in Political Science, I believe with an emphasis in Russian and Eastern European Studies. This is the department she was appointed to as a director in the National Security council. Not to mention she was appointed advisor to the Joint Chiefs of staff while in her Professorship of Political Science at Stanford.

Secretary Rice at the helm of foreign affairs took on the idea of expanding democratic governments as well as "transformational diplomacy;" she was an advocate of deploying US ambassadors to places of social, political, and economic unrest, as well as a supporter of nations combatting such issues as human and sex trafficking, and drug import/export. I can remember when I was in graduate school myself, there was a picture in one of my online textbooks, of Secretary Rice and Actress Angelina Jolie sitting on some council for these very issues.

The same old fight with Iran, Secretary Rice enforced UN sanctions on Iran until their Uranium proliferation efforts were curbed. Secretary Rice then turned her head to deal with North Korea as they sought to test their nuclear weapons. Opposed to bilateral talks with one a nation part of the "axis of evil" she welcomed them to consider the diplomatic forum composed of the six nations: China, Japan, Russia, South Korea, North Korea, and the USA. On the flip side of negative use of nuclear power and energy, one of Secretary Rice's greatest diplomatic achievements was brokering or negotiating the US-India Peace treaty which would permit trade of nuclear energy between the two nations.

59

Chapter 44

Barak Obama

President Barak Obama, first African-American President of the United States of America. This particular section may be a bit controversial for me to write onLY because during the inception of President Obama being elected and sworn into office, according to my recollection, I was literally going crazy and trying to join the Marine Corps. This was around 2008. Well, the story goes, and you can catch a bit of it in the introduction of my first book, "The Writings of Antonio" Vol. I, but I wasn't in my right mind, and end up spending about a year of my life in a Correction facility and the Psychiatric Hospital. Upon my discharge, Barak Obama was President and everything seemed a little different when I got out. In the ramp up before the election, and before I was unwell, I can remember the emotions I felt about the potential of an African-American male President, myself being an African-American male. I was a young man, with a new family, doing ministry and not knowing much about politics, just gleaning from things I saw and heard from those around me and television. My first reaction honestly was a little perturbed because there was a rumor going around my job that Barak "Hussain" Obama, was a Muslim. I hadn't done much research myself and found myself having to defend a presidential candidate whom I didn't even know if I supported yet, just because he was African American.

Later there were conversations with my own Father, an adamant Obama supporter, as I lived in Phoenix, Arizona and heard of Barak being young and without military service, I was thinking that McCain might be a better candidate because of his military background and might be a bit tougher on our enemies given the climate in Iraq and Afghanistan. Turns out, President Barak Obama did just fine on that note, ordering the hit on Osama Bin Laden, and continued to protect our nation dutifully with intellect, business acumen, social justice, national pride, Force, and Rigor. Ok, that's what I remember, I end up reading a few of his books and books written on his ideals by other so called "experts" or "critics," and all I can recall from that material and from what I hear from most people I speak to is that Obama was extremely liberal and promoted a Socialist Agenda. What that exactly means, I'm not quite sure but I don't think he was as liberal socially as let's say Bernie Sanders, or some of the other democratic candidates who were on the docket this up and coming election year.

Alright, I'm still spit balling, and then on to the official write-up, but I remember that controversy over President Barak Obama elect having to disassociate himself from his then Pastor Jeremiah Wright. A fiery Black Minister with a major church in Chicago. I guess the argument was that Barak Obama, the future President should not be associated with "black hate speech." I could be wrong, but Pastor Jeremiah Wright was a Christian minister, and not along the lines of let's say, a Luis Farrakhan. Honestly, I haven't heard many speeches or sermons from either, but the point is, I thought the whole ordeal interesting and not sure if necessary to prove if the Chief Commander of a nation is not being led by another influencer with an overly social agenda.

Other than these things, the last thing I remember from a book I read by Obama, I think maybe, "I Believe," as he talked about his process of running for the Precedency, and that it was his pure dislike in having to make phone calls and ask high dollar sponsors, supporters, philanthropist, actors and the such for financial backing and support to his cadency. For some reason this resonates with me today as I think about trying to boost my book sales and as I read marketing literature, many sources talk about having lists, and biting the bullet and making those type calls and connects in order to be successful. AAaaargh...the dread. I rather just write, and publish the books and somehow hope they magically get discovered and take off. Maybe, digitally or something. Anyway, enough of me, back to President Barak Obama.

So, Barak Obama was educated at the Colombia University. I think it goes without saying that

President Obama was born in Hawaii, to his White American mother and Kenyan Father. He went on to graduate from Law School at Harvard and also held the position of President and editor of the class newspaper. Then. afterward he also did community work with neighborhood churches in Chicago and ultimately taught Constitutional Law at Columbia. Before his ascension to the presidency he served as a United States Senator.

In terms of Foreign policy there was the never-ending mess in Iraq and Afghanistan that President Obama would pull troops out of in an attempt to bring our service members home, and yet we found ourselves drawn back into building and protecting nations overseas as well as training their men to police and guard their own cities in the face of the insurgency and violent Muslim extremist.

A new enemy arose during the Presidency of Obama, that of ISIS (The Islamic State of Iraq and Syria), and which Obama would order numerous airstrikes for their massive disruptions of terror and ethnic cleansing. Despite plans to withdraw all troops and end the war by August of 2010, US troops remained overseas in great number in the realm of over 40,000, including transitional troops and re-enforcements; still fighting, as well as training, equipping, and advising Iraqi's own homeland security force.

In terms of US troop presence in Afghanistan, it was the same story because of the unfortunate nature of the events, US leadership felt it wise to maintain military personnel in Afghanistan indefinitely after multiple vacillations of wanting to bring servicemen and women home permanently to ramping up deployed numbers aggressively.

President Barak Obama's dealings with Israel were involved to say the least. He took a stand for an Arab-Israeli independent dual state, and yet was known to say in so many words, and I paraphrase, "Nothing will ever break the bond between the US and Israel." And also, again in so many words, "Supporting Israel is consistent with the values that I've known all throughout my career since I've been politically conscious." He did pose slight challenge to Prime Minister Netanyahu as he began to expand Israeli territory throughout the West Bank. Likewise Benjamin Netanyahu voiced his disappointment in President Obama signing the Iran Nuclear deal calling it in so man words a massive threat.

In Lybia, on the side of the people and against the dictator Muammar Gaddafi, President Obama, in risk of being constitutionally sound, ordered Airstrikes in order to protect Libyan citizens and to help topple Gaddafi and his militias and dictator government.

In terms of Syria, in the months after the inception of the civil war turmoil, President Barak Obama delegated the CIA and Pentagon to train Anti-Assad rebel forces to do their various tactical bidding which unfortunately proved to be unsuccessful, as chemical weapons were released on the civilians of

Syria. I can imagine there was spy craft involved, sabotage, disinformation, tactical missions conducted, a long with propaganda, but who knows, this may be coming from a guy whose seen to many Hollywood blockbuster's or is it Netflix these days, and read to many spy novels. On that note, might as well plug my own Spy Novel Book entitled, "How Scott Walker Became a Spy, Ghost Writer Spy Novel Series Vol. I" Not to get off topic, these were very serious matters happening in Syria; loss of life, civil unrest, corruption of government, and leadership, and all-out War.

As aforementioned, President Obama was responsible for taking swift action in ordering United States Navy Seals to eliminate the target of Osama Bin Laden as intelligence report from CIA leadership;---namely Leon Panetta, check out his story in "Worthy Fights," gave report on the ascertained location of the enemy combatant after months of surveillance. Osama Bin Laden suffered by shooting death by the hand of Untied States Navy SEALs along with intelligence gathered from the compound in which he was hiding out; compute drives, discs, and various files and papers.

The first acting Secretary of State in the Obama administration was William Joseph Burns. He had a sagacious Foreign Ministry and political career of some 30 years. His education started with a B.A. in History and them on to a Masters and Doctorate In Philosophy. He served as Foreign affairs minister to Russia, expert in Near East Affairs and later as the deputy of under Secretary of State.

The First sworn in Secretary of State in President Barak Obama's administration was none other than Hillary Diane Rodham Clinton. She was a native of Chicago, Illinois and attended undergrad at Weslayen College and then Yale School of Law for her Juris Doctorate. She went on to practice on some Senatorial committee as an assistant and eventually found herself in Arkansas being an advocate for Families and Single Mothers and Children and hooked or hitched up with her Future Husband Bill, who was also an attorney at the time. Bill Clinton that is, 42 President of the United States. But this is about Hlliary, she was a New York Senator and the first women to win a party nomination for the Presidency as she achieved this feat and was a runner up against Barak Obama. I can remember watching her, Obama and John McCain verbally duke it out in present their cases and strong points of why they should be President. Later it was her and President Trump. Nevertheless, I digress, this passage is suppose to be about her role as Secretary of State in the Obama administration and her Foreign Policy decisions. In all her roles of service for the State department, before her ascension, she strongly advocated for the youth, fought teen pregnancies, implemented health care programs with veterans in mind, helped Rebuild New York after the Terrorist attacks of 9/ 11—She was a benefit to many in her position.

As Secretary of State she would respond to Benghazi attacks in Libya with military intervention. Her advocacy and actions toward this move were not fast enough apparently for United States Government Facilities being attacked by Benghazi militia according to certain Republican critics. Additionally, one of the major developments in the Obama administration and during Secretary Clinton's tenure was the idea of "Smart Power." a fusion of military intervention along with innovative diplomacy including economic policies, world health aide, and human right advocacy. This strategy was used to curb direct military action in Libya and was the initial strategy used to attempt to defuse Syrian conflict.

Other develops in the state department due to Secretary Clintons influence was the new usage of Facebook and Twitter among other Social Media sights to help get out Government messages to the people of foreign nations. She also was an advocate of Women's rights in Middle Eastern nations, where great gender inequality and even brutality existed.

John Kerry was the second official sworn in Secretary of State during the Obama nomination. Hs journey is interesting as he came from a military family and attended boarding school in Massachusetts. I had the opportunity to read one of his books and honestly main points that I remember is that he graduated with a MBA from Harvard or one of the Ivy leagues, made some money by investing in stocks and was High ranking religious leader in the Mormon Church. Turns out that my memory is horrible because it was a Juris dorctorate that he earned form Boston College, and his undergraduate degree was in political science from Yale. He was also was combat ready during the Vietnam era, he enlisted in the Navy Reserve as an Officer in Charge (OIC) and was honored for his courage in service as he was awarded a few metals for his time and service as he manned a Swift Boat.

Other leadership positions held by John Kerry before his position of Secretary of State was his Assistant to the District Attorney Office position, as well as him serving as senator of Massachusetts. Coincidentally, or should I say ironically, John Kerry was very outspoken about his stand against the War in Vietnam after he returned home from combat. Also, he was a critic of President Bush's initial response to Iraq, opposing the war in Iraq, as John Kerry was a runner up for the 2004 election.

In terms of actual foreign policy decisions developed and carried out, Secretary Kerry was adamantly in support of military intervention in the case of "Syria's despot and corrupt government leadership" using chemical weapons. against the Ghouta suburbs of Damascus. Eventually talks between US, Russia and the rest of the UN community would convince Syrian Leader Bashar al-Assad, to give up his stock pile of chemical weapons and Syria would also apply for membership to the UN Council, agreeing to US and Russian destruction of 100% of Syrian chemical weapon arsenal.

60

61

Chapter 45

Donald J. Trump

President Donald J. Trump sits incumbent, as of this June of

2020, the 45thPresident of the United States of America. And in the midst of all the controversy, it appears that Mr. Trump serves as a capable and competent President, handling Foreign Policy matters, Negotiating, Vetoing and Implementing Sanctions, Tariffs deals with hostile nations and Congress, dealing in War, and appealing to the economic woes of the American people by approving advantages economic stimulus packages in the midst of the recent and ongoing COVID-19 attacks.

I'll take a moment to spitball here, and then on with the official write=up. I really didn't know much about Trump before he was in office. I grew up not watching a huge amount of television so I only heard about His aggressive personality and him "firing " people on his hit show, "The Apprentice." Then there were the side jokes about "Where was Obama born?" and wanting to see his Birth

Certificate." I had obviously heard he was a Billionaire with Hotels and Golf Courses, and suddenly He's running for President on the Republican Ticket. Debates with Hillary, comments about Emails and mishandleling things with Syria or Benghazi, I think...And then he was President.

There were the harsh comments about Mexican Immigrants all being "rapists and murderers" and the "Shit hole" comment about some place in Africa or Haiti. And the comment about there being "Good people" on both sides referring to those protestors of Black Lives Matter and the Neo Nazis. And suddenly, America is in political uproar. Excessive police brutality, murders, and even riots and looting amidst peaceful protests in certain cities. Things got crazy. And yet, I would consider myself still asleep to the hurtful reality of subtle, institutional, systemic and stratified racism in America that marginalize people of color, because it was not my daily reality. Maybe when I was in jail, but even that gave me certain privileges. So, as a Black American Male, or American Male of African Descent, I stand sorrowful and grieved for all that I hear and see. But my motive is not to dwell there, yet not ignore the pain of the people, yet not necessarily promote it either. Go figure, sometimes it's just too depressing and seems to be same old story to talk about these themes I studied in college, and I rather focus on other topics of productivity than be stagnant in the history of injustice and hateful crimes. Yet, we must to move forward.

Now, how do I clean this up? I come from a military family, and at one point, wanted to be a Marine myself, hence my time. So, I have no problem with hard talk and even cocky Police doing their job. It's when the line of injustice and honor of duty is forsaken that there should be consequences. Some that have read my first book may have picked up on the fact that I do landscaping on the side; well, one of my clients is an old Marine who served in Vietnam, and I was asking him what he thought about all the commotion about Trump and him supposedly getting Russia to interfere with elections. He wisely and astutely told me that it was a "Privileged conversation between Heads of State." Weather it was legal or impeachable, I did not quite know or even care, or want an impeachment to happen; unlike so many critics of the man, I thought he was doing a decent enough job. The whole circus and I should be careful, because I have not read any reports or testimony's from FBI agents, but seemed to simply be a lethal exercise of legal "push=ups" and pull-ups(NPR Radio).

Suddenly, there was the dealings with Iran and the executing of General Solemani, and this is right about when I started to wake up a little more to Society, Politics, and sort of what was going on. I was tuned into the after briefing and it seemed like President Trump and Secretary of State Mike Pompeo were doing a Yeomen's job of preemptive strike and sustaining pressure on Iran through Sanctions in retaliation for Iran's airstrike. Of course, next came the Covid-19 "accidental" or covert strike from China; and from a civilians perspective, I thought handling and implementation of certain economic programs and policies were handled in good timely fashion. Being a small business owner myself, I received a small PPP Loan through my Navy Federal Credit Union, after several attempts of going to a few other institutions and running into roadblocks. I did not consider these blocks as racial or even racist, but simply a challenge to me to be a better businessman.

In terms of books I've read on President Trump, I read somewhere that He's written fourteen. I read one where He interviewed a bunch of wealthy people and gained wisdom from how they made it. All I can remember from that book is that if someone offers you a loan, take It! Of course such philosophy fly's in the face of good Christian wisdom which suggests that we are to be the loaners and not the borrowers, and clearing ourselves forum debts. Except that Christ says "Make friends with those of unrighteous mammon." (Luke 16:9). Who knows? And then I just recently purchased, "The Art of the Deal," from Amazon, and have not yet made my way all the way through it, but seems that President Trump was an busy, productive, and Industrious young man—not to mention ambitious.

Okay, those are my thoughts, here comes the official part. President Trump is from Queens, New York and majored in Economics as an undergrad, obtaining his degree from The Wharton School, a private Ivy League school in Pennsylvania. He attended a military Academy during his adolescent years. After graduating with his Bachelor's degree went on to expand the family Luxury Real Estate Business and even saw himself in Television as aforementioned.

In terms of Foreign policy matters, President Trump approaches Foreign policy decisions with a unilateral ideology in mind, protecting America First, majoring on US defense spending and minoring on NATO spending. Middle Eastern affairs found more chemical weapons deployed near Damascus by Syrian leadership and President Trump ordered execution of corrupt government leadership there as well as airstrikes in retaliation.

There seemed to be some wires that got crossed between President Trumps announcement and willingness to pull US Troops out of harm's way in Syria. Apparently This precipitated the resignation of Mattis who was concerned about Kurdish allies and intelligence gathered by the Department of Defense. Soon, National Security Advisor John Bolton would announce that US forces would stay in Syria until ISIS insurgent forces fully rooted out and mission executed to completion; along with an agreement from Turkey to no longer strike American Kurdish Allies.

We made money with Saudi Arabia in an 110 Billion Dollar Deal sealing them Arms. President Trump increased Military presence in Afghanistan by some 6000 troops and contradicted or vetoed any ideas of "Negotiating with Terrorist or the Taliban," even if it was to attempt to Force them into settlement.

Moreover, around 2017 attacks on Saudi Arabia, our Allies along with the United Arab Emirates led President Trump to deploy troops to that area for protection of as well as issue Bombers to the Persian Gulf along with a carrier group of Navy Force in retaliation against what was suspected to be Iranian aggression.

When it comes to Israel, President Trump recognized Jerusalem as the capital and opened a US Embassy in the city against the council of the UN which developed a policy against "diplomatic missions" in the Holy City. There were other matters of acknowledging Israel's annexation of Golan Heights that was also heavily criticized by the Arab League and the EU.

Since 2017, Hard language had come from President Trump as he faced North Korea's leadership threatening their existence if they intended to do harm to US or any of its allies. North Korea persisted in their morbid cause, boasting about their testing a Super Weapon. Eventually Kim Jun Un would stand down; in light of multiple Sanctions on the nation and the denuclearization talks with President Trump, progress was made; if only Kim Jun Un would stick to his word.

When it comes to Russia, US relations were not good at first, even when viewing the Saga of the Cold War at a glance. President Trump was observant and gave no praise to Russia's actions in Syria, Ukraine, and Venezuela. On the contrary, President Trump thanked Russian leader Vladimir

Putin, after certain US officials were fired from American Embassy in Russia. For what reason, I am uncertain.

Trade relations are restricted to Cuba under President Trump's administration. His thinking is that this will impeded upon economic resources flowing to Cuban military, business, and intelligence Agencies. This ideology is a change in policy from outgoing President Obama's policy which loosened trade relations with Cuba.

And then there is Venezuela, President Trump has not completely dismissed the idea of Military action to get a hold of the rampant Socialist, and bankrupt nation. With astronomical inflation and decreased value of the currency, a hurt Monduro was angered at President's Trumps acknowledging of Juan Guido's leadership instead of himself, an opposition leader to the current socialist, and corrupt government.

Foreign relations with China have been Tumultuous to say the least. Tariffs and Sanctions have been enforced, and yet million dollar trade deals have been made. Currently Chinese government and it's police force in Hong Kong project a brutal image of injustice as ordinary citizens are harassed, beaten, and terrorized by their own governing officials under National Security Law. Human rights issues were in jeopardy as Hong Kong forces manage crowds of protestors and common citizens.

Finally, in consideration of NATO, as a runner up, President Trump stated that evolution would need to happen within the organization for US to maintain the same commitment with him at the helm. As president, US still retains the right to act unilaterally, and the President wants All NATO members to essentially pay their equal share of dues.

The First acting Secretary of State in the Trump administration was Thomas A. Shannon. He served in two acting capacities in the Trump administration; that is Deputy Secretary of state and Under Secretary of Political Affairs. He earned his bachelor's degree in Government and Politics, and went on to get a Masters and Ph.D in philosophy at the University of Oxford.

The first sworn in Secretary of State in the Trump administration was Rex Tillerson. He was an American Engineer and Businessman. He served on various conglomerate business boards as Chair and was the CEO of ExxonMobil. a company in the top ten wealthiest companies with respect to revenue. Former Secretary Rex Tillerson came to President Trump as a recommendation by Former Secretary Condoleezza Rice of the Bush administration and served for approximately one year until the swearing in of incumbent Secretary of State, Mike Pompeo, former CIA director.

On Secretary Tillerson's first Foreign Affairs visit in Bonn, Germany, he met with foreign leaders of the G20 and relayed US special interest and willingness toward those missions and its allies. Russia in particular was advised to stand down from her War efforts in the Ukraine, and that in return US would cooperate with Russia on "Practical Matters" that would benefit the American people. Holding Russia to its Minsk Agreement to scale down its violence in the Ukraine.

Later talks with Mexico were concerns of border security, arms trafficking, and migration. Then there were the trips to the far east, Japan, Korea, and China. Secretary Tillerson's assessed was basically, in so many words that there may be a preemptive strike necessary coming to North Korea if they evert brought harm to US forces, or Ally, South Korea and in addition refuse to stop it's ramping up of weaponizing itself with nuclear power to a level of international danger, then US military force would meet this aggression with appropriate response.

Finally, there was a report written entitled "Trafficing impersons Report" which monitors and combats human trafficking by listing governments for their acknowledgement and "perceived" efforts to stop human trafficking in their specified territories. Apparently, Secretary Tillerson's report had the oversight of excluding Afghanistan, Myanmar, and Iraq; countries with this problem of employing child soldiers.

Incumbent Secretary of State Mike Pompeo is essentially who, in his and President's Trump's reporting on next moves in Iran after the elimination of Iranian General Qasem Soleimani, Inspired this work. I was tuned into various online news streaming and reporting and suddenly realized my ignorance to all that's really been going on in the world, especially with respect to foreign policy decisions and US engagements to protect our nation. I mean I had read a few books and all, but really hadn't been keeping current with the reality of terrorist threats weather at home or abroad on our bases, Embassies, and ground troops, global insurgency, ISIS. China, North Korea and other Communist and Socialist regimes. So, I thought writing this book would be an attempt for me and others to get up to speed as well as document some history and perspective. Even though as I sit writing now, my memory already fades. Go Figure.

Notwithstanding, Secretary Mike Pompeo was born in Kansas and played Basketball in High School. He went on to the The Military Academy at West Point and graduated with a degree in Engineering Management. From there it was off to join the United States Army where he toured in Germany, ranked as an executive Sqaudren Officer and eventually Captain upon discharge. Next came Law school at Harvard Law where he earned a juris doctorate, and came back to Kansas to become councilmen in the House of Representatives and eventually director of the CIA after also working for a private law firm in Washington.

In 2018, Secretary Pompeo was influential in talks with North Korea at the summit in Singapore to recover bodies of old soldier remains from Korean War. He was critical of concentration camps in China of the minority Muslim population there as well as Iran's leader Ayatollah Ali Khamenei for their lack of urgency in not persecuting China for such terror against their fellow Muslims. Today in 2020, Secretary Pompeo continues to be critical of Chinese Communist Party (CCP) and their mistreatment of citizens and Human Rights abuse in Hong Kong.

Talks of and with Israel and it's leadership was well, as Secretary Pompeo suggested that Israel was essentially a model that US would like all of the Middle East to follow. Secretary Pompeo remains a firm supporter of Israel, also being a Christian leader himself. Furthermore, he stated that Israel-US relations are, "stronger than ever." January of 2019, US troops were moved from Syria, and yet Secretary Pompeo, commending the fight, relayed to Middle Eastern nations that US mission to disrupt and destroy ISIS insurgency would not and had not change.

In terms of Venezuela, in the same vein as President Trump, Secretary Pompeo officially announced Juan Guaidó as the new leader of the nation, to the dismay of Monduro.

Talks with Russia in May of 2019 surrounded around the New Strategic Arms Reduction Treaty (New START) in addition to nations such as Iran, North Korea, China, and Venezuela.

Moreover, today 2020, Secretary Pompeo continues to expose China for their tyranny and authoritarian government that seeks to pit Europe in choosing between Democracy and the Free world and essentially Communism and Authoritarian governments way of life. We see China's actions with Hong Kong, Taiwan, the pacific Islands, India and even Malaysia. Ultimately, China threatens herself is she suggest military movement against the United States, as our forces stand ready, though we be deeply intertwined.

Presently the executive branch and State department combat COVID-19 on a national level among other economic matters. President Trump along with members of his cabinet relayed strategic plans to isolate the virus through social distancing and careful washing of hands, face masks, and an increase in financial support for certain companies for the manufacturing of ventilators, such as Ford and GM. Other efforts in the in the Bio-Tech sector or industry; FDA regulations have been relaxed so that Bioitech companies can roll out their vaccines sooner than later, allowing speedy human trials and the skipping of animal testing phases. Companies that foresee their vaccines being ready for mass distribution this year are: Moderna (MRNA), and AstraZeneca (AZN). Later, will come, Invio (INO), Pfizer (PFE), not to mention Johnson and Johnson (JNJ).

-The End, For Now -

Note from Author:

Greetings Everyone... Thanks for reading, Hope you enjoyed my note taking and bursts of commentary here and there. I'm no political science major nor am I a lawyer with political aspirations. I am just a curious civilian with a thirst for knowledge and a desire to understand how things work, and to ultimately benefit economically from these self-interests. Of course, there is also the dreamy idea that knowledge will spread abroad and that it would make us all a more informed, understanding, more intelligent and less hateful people. I hope you will come along and check out my fourth book in this Volume series."The Writings of Antonio Vol. IV (The Parables of Christ; His Dark Sayings)." I said that I would jump from spiritual to secular topics, with spy novels, fantasy, and sci-fi coming soon. There goes my ambition. We'll see if it gets done. LOL.

To Follow and See other Books by Antonio go to: amazon.com/author/antonio.

(To get to author page, type in link just as, period at the end included.).

ANTONIO A. SWEENEY

The Writings of Antonio

Vol. IV

(The Parables of Christ; His Dark Sayings)

62

Dedicated To:

To those who Hear and Believe,

And want their Eyes Opened;

To Those who Wonder if;

the Things Christ said be True or,

Have Meaning Yesterday, Today

and Throughout the Eternal Ages.

And To My Kids,

Imani, Nathan, Ophelia, and Sonia

And to my

Wife

And he said, Go, and tell this people, Hear ye indeed,

but understand not; and see ye indeed, but perceive not.

Make the heart of this people fat, and make their ears heavy,

and shut their eyes; lest they see with their eyes, and hear with their ears, and understand with their heart, and convert, and be healed.

- *Isiaah 6:9-10*

Whom shall he teach knowledge? and whom shall he make

to understand doctrine? them that are weaned from the milk,

and drawn from the breasts.

For precept must be upon precept, precept upon precept;

line upon line, line upon line; here a little, and there a little:

For with stammering lips and another tongue will he speak

to this people.

To whom he said, This is the rest wherewith ye may cause

the weary to rest; and this is the refreshing: yet they would

not hear.

-Isiah (28:11-13).

References:

1. https://en.wikipedia.org/wiki/List_of_Secretaries_of_State_of_the_United_States

2. https://history.state.gov/departmenthistory/people/secretaries

3. https://www.whitehouse.gov/about-the-white-house/presidents/

Introduction

God made it that his Son bear witness of Him. He is a Great King and Ruler of Heaven and Earth and His Son; Christ that is, is Lord of All, and yet they are One of the same heart and of the same Spirit, Invisible, Triune in One, until the Father reveal the Son. And if His maxims upon the earth were true, then let US go and Understand the Words of God incarnate, more specifically, the Words taught by Christ in parables as he dwelled among us.

As Lord, he gave fundamental principles, business and spiritual principles for our temporal and eternal success. May he also give us understanding that the eyes of our minds and hearts may be open to his Words and thoughts clearly, that our lives may change for the better or that we may stand and think upon what He has said unto us and evaluate what it means for us and the World we live in today, thousands of year later, and beyond.

The word Parable, comes from the Greek word παραβολή - parabole, in the Greek; Which carries the meaning of placing two things along side one another or in juxtaposition as ships in battle. Further connotation suggests comparing two things with one another to determine likeness or similitude. Another way a parable can be used is as a narrative weather fictitious or true, that relays precept or principle concerning the nature of God and His Kingdom, Man and His Behavior, thus figuratively speaking of literal matters. Christ angles His parables to make use of all three of these methods, thereby explaining his principles of the Kingdom in dark sayings to be understood by all who hear and have an intelligent ear to listen, and mind to investigate.

In the Hebrew the word Parable is ?????? – mashal; which has more so the meaning of proverb, maxim, aphorism, or wise and ethical sentence. The proverbs of Solomon and some of the Psalms come to mind, as well as the many lines in the prophetic scriptures. So, we see that all throughout the bible, stories are told; lines and sentences fall from heaven upon the ears of holy men moved by the Holy Spirit to write and speak these divine truths. It is not to say that every ready writer or Preacher who expounds upon the Words of God are giving inspired and inerrant words to live on, for quite the contrary, the scripture sayeth, "prophesies, they shall fail" (1Co 13:8), and warns us to "test the spirit" (1Jo 4:1). The word test used here is actually try or δοκιμάζω – dokimazō, and means to test, try, scrutinize, determine if genuine, as in the way metals are tested to determine their worth.

There are 40 parables, and dark sayings as we are calling them and I am recording and expounding upon. 40 being a number of testing, for it rained for 40 days and 40 nights during the Ancient Flood during the time of Noah. Moses stayed on top of the mountain communing with God 40 days, and 40 nights receiving and writing the Commandments of God upon tablets, and Christ himself after he was Baptized went into the desert fasting without food or water for 40 days and 40 nights to be tempted of the Devil. The first three Kings of Israel reigned for 40 years each; Saul, David, and Solomon. Ironically, and without any planning on my part, I begin writing this book in my 39th year upon the Earth, prayerfully to make it to my 40th Birthday in December and beyond in the Blessed favor of God.

To highlight this herein format that I will follow in this book; similar to the format rolled out in the previous volumes; Vol. I and II in particular, there will be an introduction to each parable, the scripture text of the actual dark saying, including its chapter verse location, and then interpretation and commentary. Thank you for Reading, Enjoy!

-Antonio A. Sweeney MS

June, 2020

Chapter 1

"Light Under a Bushel"

Greetings Friend and Reader--This first parable that we will discuss, maybe you have heard many times before, or have not heard it exactly, but be familiar with the idea of not "hiding your light" or "Letting your Light Shine." Immediately, this notion has the potential to present inner conflict and a feeling of uneasiness for those among us who be introverts and prefer the inner life and maybe even a withdrawn from people and society lifestyle. I believe, Light here in this context, as Christ talks about it can have several meanings; not just the primary one we may all be thinking of, that is the enthusiasm, or power of the Holy Spirit shining through us,--that is the Spirit of Christ himself, living and manifesting Himself through our works, speech and actions. This, I believe is the light we can choose either to display or hide. A mystery of righteousness to the mystery of iniquity, in that God Incarnate dwells within us.

Yet, there is more. What is light really? I mean, what is the Scientific definition of light. Well, I can vaguely remember High School Chemistry and Physics, and then there was the repeat and more in-depth lessons in College on the same Topic; but what is light as we know it; not only from a spiritual, metaphysical , and even eastern/ middle-eastern perspective; but a scientific one. I'm not talking about auras and halos, but understanding light as a physical chemical concept, understood by every scientist; as an Electro—magnetic wave. And that's the thing that I slightly I remember about light, is that, it has two components; or is made of two waves, Electo and Magnetic. The Electrical component of light, and how we see visible light comes from oscillating elections that move very rapidly and are charged and upon their release of those charges, and/ or returning to its resting place; they emit what are called "photons of light." Kind of like an action potential in a nerve cell or that electoral signal that keeps the heart beating, only this is electrical and not biochemical.

The point is, light has many components; wavelength, colors, speed, and frequencies both visible and invisible, And I believe part of what Christ is saying to us today in this parable is that as mankind, we first off, have light in US. We just learned that light has many components and consist of electro-magnetic waves, consisting of oscillating electrons that emit photons of light at various frequencies, both visible and invisible. Well, how does this translate? As people, we function on different levels or frequencies, sometimes we are high strung, other times we are low key, and then for the normal and un-diagnosed in society, sometimes we maintain a baseline functionality that is quite visible and apparent to the people and world around us. Likewise, with Light, radio waves are slower and you can't see them, Gamma rays are faster and also cannot be seen as well as Infared rays. These all fall under the spectrum of electromagnetic waves, which is known as light.

Have you ever seen someone's eyes turn red, and I mean not in a picture. What about the spark of light, or bright and starry look when someone's eyes "lite up" with excitement, or love and affection. How about someone with darkness in their eyes. I'm sure those of us with discernment have seen the spectrum But the point we are trying to convey is that Christ was telling the people back then and even today, that there is Light in our vessels; There is Light in US. Visible, Invisible, Moving, Oscillating, able to bring Clarity and Vision, and Safety and even Electro-Magnetic Power to our given situation. We do not have to remain in darkness. The Darkness of ignorance or the Darkness of Hate. Christ said of himself, "I am the light of the World." (John 9:5), and if that light dwell in you, in us, how shall we hide in darkness.

Now of course, there are practical concerns, I'm not saying that everyone go and be a motor mouth or high beam flash light spotting on everybody we meet, but that we simply and humbly display the works and light of God in us through are daily walk and speech upon the Earth. The Gregarious, will do their exploits, we are all gifted in various ways in capacities, one shows the light of God in what they say, another in what they've done, but in it all, Christ is encouraging us to show the Works of God and bring light to the House. The house being our

Families, our Cities, Nation and the World at large. I'll Record;

Ye are the light of the world. A city that is set on a hill cannot be hid.

Neither do men light a candle, and put it under a bushel, but on a candlestick; and it giveth light unto all that are in the house.

Let your light so shine before men, that they may see your good works, and glorify your Father which is in heaven. (Matthew:5:14-16)

And he said unto them, Is a candle brought to be put under a bushel, or under a bed? and not to be set on a candlestick?

For there is nothing hid, which shall not be manifested; neither was any thing kept secret, but that it should come abroad. (Mark 4:21-22)

So, I've recorded this parable as listed in both Mathew and Mark. A variation of it is also in the gospel of Luke; (8:16; 11:33). And given these words a closer look, it appears that Christ is also referring to the exposing power of light. Light, in and of itself, expels darkness, vanishes shadows, and helps us get a clear look at who we really are. This goes against our natural tendencies, I mean, we spend our time covering ourselves up with different identities and language, and clothing, music, careers, and the such in order to protect ourselves from being exposed. I mean, really, who wants to be exposed, or "Come into the light" when their work is too sensitive, our sins to great, and you don't know who's watching you. But Christ didn't say, "come into the light", that was from the end of the movie with Keanu Reeves fighting a fictional Gabriel Character, Hollywood's spin on making The biblical Arch Angel Gabriel who stands in the presence of God; Evil;-- "Constantine"(2005). Nevertheless, Christ said in so many words, "Be the Light or let the light in you, Shine" Love covers a multitude of sins, and surely we have the Love of God though Christ toward us. All one can do is to become the one they were or whom God created them to be, that is display the light given to you.

The biblical word light in the Greek is καίω – kaio; and carries the meaning; to set on fire, flame burning, to consume with fire. This is very different from how we understand light today, given the discovery of electricity and light switches. Back in that day, remember, they didn't have light switches or even light bulbs, their lights were fires and, boring oil lamps, and candlesticks. They understood light in a different sense than us; notwithstanding, they understood, light was powerful and necessary. There was a cleansing power to light that burns, or fire that consumes. The fire of God's spirt in them resonated with His words, and they knew that they could be guided by the flame of God inside of them, as we can be yet guided by the consuming fire that is in our life. This is the flame or heat we are to display; the fire of Christ.

What does that mean? well in Ancient Israel they also understood Light from a the perspective of Sun light, and of course there is the Genesis account of

God putting into the sky the heavenly bodies and stars for signs and seasons. Even today, we will find that we now understand the speed of light 3.0 106m/s, the time it takes for the Earth to rotate around the Sun (the greater light) and the tme it takes for the moon (the lesser light) to rotate around the Earth.

So, what am I saying? Let's look at the word Light in Hebrew when referring to the Sun, and when God said, Let there be Light, as we know in the Beginning the Earth was formless and void, and the Spirit of God moved upon the face of the Earth. God said, let there be light: ???? - 'owr, is the Hebrew lettering and pronunciation, and this word carries several additional meanings than just burning or fire. Strongs records this in the Hebrew for light, as referring to day light and the heavenly luminaries.; it refers to the light of prosperity, the face, instruction, light, lamp and that Jehovah is Israel's light.

So be a luminary; be a star or a planet, a sun, or a moon. And as you move and traverse around the earth or around the sun and sit high as the stars, allow the light that God has given to you to reflect and display the Glory of God that people may Praise our Father in Heaven.

God Bless and Have a Great Day.

    1.

Other Books by Antonio

The Writings of Antonio Vol. I

(Witty, Philosophical, Political and Sometimes Controversial Commentary on Scripture)

The Writings of Antonio Vol. II

(Philosophical and Political Commentary)

How Scott Walker Became A Spy

(Ghost Writer Spy Novel Series Vol. I)

Foreign

To Follow and See other Books by Antonio go to: amazon.com/author/antonio.

(To get to author page, type in link just as, period at the end included.)

www.ingramcontent.com/pod-product-compliance
Lightning Source LLC
Chambersburg PA
CBHW031252090426
42742CB00007B/422